DISTILLED

in

WASHINGTON

A HISTORY

BECKY GARRISON

FOREWORD BY CHARLES FINKEL, WINE AND BEER PIONEER

THE
History
PRESS

Published by The History Press
Charleston, SC
www.historypress.com

Front cover: Monopole High Grade Whiskey produced by the Bohemia Liquor Company (Seattle) circa 1911. *Courtesy of Keith Barnes/Bainbridge Organic Distillers. Back cover*: Cyrus Noble Saloon (Yakima) circa 1890. This saloon located on the southeast corner of Front Street and Yakima Avenue was connected to Frank Shardlow. In 1903, he replaced these wooden structures with a handsome brick structure housing multiple businesses on the first floor and hotel rooms on the second. Most of the businesses, except between 1916 and 1933, were a variety of saloons and drinking establishments until the building was demolished in the 1980s. *Courtesy of Yakima Valley Museum.*

First published 2024

Manufactured in the United States

ISBN 9781467156240

Library of Congress Control Number: 2023948365

To the late Gary Austin, founder of the Groundlings and my improv teacher from 1996 until his death on April Fools' Day 2017. He taught me to value stories over facts. For it's through the telling of our tales that we uncover the actual truths behind our words.

CONTENTS

ACKNOWLEDGEMENTS

Most likely, this book would not have happened without my fateful meeting with Charles Finkel, cofounder of Pike Brewing Company in Seattle. We met shortly after I relocated from the East Coast to the Pacific Northwest in 2014, where he introduced me to Jason Parker, the first head brewer for Pike and cofounder of Seattle-based Copperworks Distilling Company. Both men educated me on the nuances of the Pacific Northwest craft culture and afforded me connections that continue to serve me.

In particular, Parker connected me with A.J. Temple of Temple Distilling Company, whose insights and connections as secretary of the Washington Distillers Guild helped me navigate this state's current distilling scene. This book could not have come to life without the emails, phone calls and in-person meetings I had with distillers across Washington State, and I remain grateful to all who gifted me with their time to speak about their craft.

Also, thanks to those Oregon-based distillers I met while reporting on the Pacific Northwest craft culture. Christian Krogstad (Westward Whiskey), Christine Hopkins (Aimsir Distilling), Molly Troupe (Freeland Spirits), Ryan Csanky (Aria Gin) and Joe O'Sullivan (Hood River Distillers) answered my inquiries in a kind and patient manner, no matter how silly or inane my question might have been.

A special thank you to the State of Washington Tourism, the Washington State Wine Commission and the Northwest Cider Association, along with Washington State's local Convention and Visitor Bureaus (CVBs), historical societies and local libraries. In particular, I'm grateful to Leonard Garfield, executive director of the Museum of History & Industry (MOHAI), for taking the time to help me nuance a few lingering historical questions. Without their kind assistance, this would be a pamphlet and not a completed book with unique photographs gleaned from their carefully curated collections.

Laurie Krill, Zoe Ames, Jenni Tyler and the rest of the team at The History Press have been an absolute delight and joy in helping make this book a reality.

Finally, thanks to Thor.pdx for being a faithful traveling companion and photographer whose work and ongoing presence enabled me to capture the spirits of the Pacific Northwest.

Cheers!

FOREWORD

It took about 2,000 years for distillation to make it from Alexandria, Egypt, to what became Washington State and almost 250 years for someone to write a book about it. No one is better suited for such a task than Becky Garrison.

I first met Becky when she interviewed me for an article on craft beer. An accomplished journalist, Becky studied theology at Yale. She was in town to expose, in print, a nefarious con man, a preacher, who used church money to buy his own book to place it on the bestseller list. If Becky's soul was in religion, I could tell at our first meeting that her heart was in drinks, fermented and distilled. As she says: "With this book, I seem to have made the formal shift from covering the Holy Spirit to distilled spirits, a move that saved both my soul and my sanity."

To say that Becky herself is spirited is an understatement! An exhaustive researcher and entertaining writer, she shares the fascinating journey of pioneer distillers, from the East Coast with the landing of the *Mayflower* to Oregon Territory, later Washington Territory and, in 1889, to Washington State, the only state named for a distiller. Her "truth is stranger than fiction" account is full of never previously revealed details about everything from early fur traders who used their "hooch" to trade with the natives to the Hudson Bay Company distillery in Fort Vancouver, now Washington. She writes about pioneer distillers all over the state who metaphorically fueled mining operations here and beyond and about local distillers supplying a growing metropolis.

Above: Jason Parker, Copperworks Distilling Company (*left*), and Charles Finkel, Pike Brewing Company (*right*). *Courtesy of Thor.pdx.*

Opposite: Spiked Stout. Ingredients: Copperworks Single Malt Whiskey, cinnamon simple syrup, egg whites, Pike Kilt Lifter Scotch Ale reduction and Pike 5X Stout. Garnished with fresh grated cinnamon. *Courtesy of Austin Sconce, former Pike Innovative Specialist, Pike Brewing Company.*

We learn that as good as business was, as the nineteenth turned into the twentieth century, distilling was facing an uphill battle with the headwinds of the temperance movement, itself fueled by nefarious preachers and their Anti-Saloon League. Garrison reports that, delivering on prophecy, liquor sales were made illegal in Washington State in 1916. The whole country followed, prohibiting sales and most consumption in 1920. Garrison writes that during Prohibition, illicit whiskey was available—plus, you could get a prescription for a pint of bourbon, or if your spirits were down, obtain them from your priest or rabbi.

I learned that after repeal in 1933, the state Liquor Control Board took over not only regulating spirits but selling them, too, purposely discouraging consumption. The author tells a lurid tale of corruption in government and organized crime. We learn about kickbacks on whiskey at the highest levels of the liquor board—alas, not on local whiskey. Local distilleries didn't have a prayer until the state gave up control. For anyone who loved single malts, gin, vodka, amaro, rye, rum, brandy, bourbon, cordials and other coveted craft concoctions, it was heavenly news when the state stores and antiquated laws were voted out.

The story of how a craft-distilling renaissance began and hasn't stopped yet is fantastic reading. Vignettes about distillers like Don Poffenroth and Kent Fleischmann, who launched Dry Fly Distilling in 2007, making it the state's first craft distiller; Jason Parker at Copperworks, our first head brewer at Pike; Matt Hoffman at Westland, who loved single malt so much he went to Heriot-Watt University in Edinburgh, Scotland, to learn how to make it; Orlin Sorensen and Brett Carlile at Woodinville Whiskey, who crafted so fine a bourbon that their company was purchased by France's luxury leader LVMH; and scores of other alchemists, artists and adventurous entrepreneurs make this a book that is hard to put down.

I give thanks to Becky Garrison for a work of genius. You will, too, after reading *Distilled in Washington: A History*.

Charles Finkel

Charles Finkel is a designer, entrepreneur, artist and founder of Bon-Vin, Merchant du Vin and Pike Brewing Company in Seattle, Washington.

PREFACE

They say you never forget your first. I still remember the time when I encountered that holy trinity of fly-fishing, cigars and Scotch in the '90s. Lagavulin 16, to be precise.

Given my booze-infested family tree, I learned to be mindful of my alcohol consumption. But Lagavulin 16 taught me how to savor my liquor, not swig it as was the practice among most of my extended family members. With each sip, I prayed to the peat and found my true salvation in Scotch.

At the time, I was a "professional Christian" writer who satirized those unbiblical bullies that chose profits over prophecy while also reporting on those grassroots ventures that helped connect people in our shared humanity. When this exploration took me from the Northeast to the Pacific Northwest in 2014, I stopped marketing myself to the "Christian industrial complex."

Instead, I began exploring the sacred sexuality and Celtic spirituality informed by the natural beauty of this region.[1] In this quest, I embraced the local craft culture with a focus on beer, cannabis/CBD, cider, distilled spirits and wine. During my reporting on the institutional church, critiques of its work were met with fervorous opposition, which I now see is common among spiritual narcissists.[2] Fortunately, I found a more welcoming spirit in brewpubs and tasting rooms. These places assumed the communal role once held by the institutional church where people came together for friendship, sponsored local fundraisers and engaged in other grassroots-y community-building endeavors.

In particular, when I began sampling this region's American single malt whiskeys, I found myself rekindling my love of Lagavulin but with a Pacific Northwest twist. With each sip of these whiskeys (as well as other craft spirits), I can almost taste what the Celts call this "thin line" that separates our world from the next. You can truly drink in the spirit of this place.

With this book, I seem to have made the formal shift from covering the Holy Spirit to distilled spirits, a move that saved both my soul and my sanity. As I continue to explore this region's craft culture, I keep meeting other like-minded spiritual seekers, who have found salvation in these spirited communities.

Cheers!

INTRODUCTION

Ever since the Pilgrims had to land at Plymouth Rock in 1620 because they ran out of beer, early settlers in this New World were saturated in alcohol.[3] Throughout the day, men, women and even children would consume beer and cider, as the water was deemed unfit to drink. Also, those with means continued to enjoy the refined spirits and wines they brought from their former homeland.

Public consumption of liquor in colonial times remained primarily a manly pursuit. Proper women consumed the beer, cider and distilled spirits they made at home. As in any kitchen, the quality of these spirits was contingent on both the cook's skill and the ingredients they could access and afford.

This new land was primarily rural, and farmers often produced a surplus of grain and fruits. Without pasteurization or refrigeration, distilling proved a viable and delectable option to preserve their harvests from rotting. A still could be found on many family farms, with farmers often supplementing their meager incomes by selling those spirits not consumed by their family and friends.

"Un début." *Courtesy of Charles Finkel, Pike Brewing Company's Microbrewery Museum.*

Left: Copper pot stills from George Washington's distillery at Mount Vernon. This faithfully reconstructed working distillery produces small batch spirits on site by replicating the distilling methods utilized by colonial-era distillers. *Courtesy of Steve Bashore, head distiller.*

Below: Copperworks Distilling Company's copper pot still imported from Scotland features some of the latest distilling technology, though this overall system remains very similar to colonial-era stills. *Courtesy of Copperworks Distilling Company.*

Despite advances in technology, the production steps involved in distilling have not changed much from these early colonial days.

～

Recipe for Moonshine

The process begins by producing alcohol through the fermentation of sugar sourced from grain, fruit or other substrates into a "mash." This mash is placed in a closed container (the still pot) and heated until an alcoholic steam is produced. This steam then escapes through an outlet at the top of the pot, passing through a pipe (the worm), which is cooled either by contact with the air or by passing through a series of tubs of cold water. The steam is recaptured as a liquid in a second closed container (the condenser). Each time a distiller follows this procedure of adding mash to the still pot, he has run off a batch, and each batch is one of a series that forms a run.[4]

75 pounds plain white cornmeal
300 pounds sugar
1 pound yeast
15 pounds bran (optional)
300 gallon water

This recipe yields approximately 48 gallons of liquor.[5]

～

This assumes everything went according to plan. *In Bourbon Empire: The Past and Present of America's Whiskey*, Reid Mitenbuler recounts George Thorpe's exploits as the "alleged" founder of the first distillery in America circa 1621 at Berkeley Plantation in Virginia. He substituted corn for barley in brewing beer and owned a small still. Given the value and popularity of spirits, there's a good chance that, at some point, he tried distilling his corn beer, though this cannot be confirmed. Also, the primitive nature of the equipment and methods sometimes prevented the magic from happening. Temperature was often an issue, and to keep the fermentation warm in cold weather, steaming manure might have been packed around the vats. If a batch resisted fermentation, it wasn't out of the question to add the carcass of a dead animal to kick-start the process.[6]

While the early settlers drank from breakfast to bedtime, their everyday lives did not resemble the Bacchanalian excesses of a Roman orgy. As Eric Burns wrote in *The Spirits of America*, "Booze was food, medicine and companionship in the early days of America: ichor, elixir and aqua vitae. It was how the tongue got loose and the mind receptive, how the body unlimbered and the future grew bright. It was a boost for one's courage, a shield against loneliness, a light in the midnight hours when the stars were hidden and the moon otherwise occupied."[7]

Even President George Washington got into the booze business. In 1799, his distillery produced just over 10,500 gallons of rye whiskey, along with a few hundred gallons of peach and apple brandy.[8]

Between 1790 and 1830, spirits consumption in the United States nearly doubled from five to nine and a half gallons per person annually.[9] According to American historian W.J. Rorabaugh, author of *The Alcoholic Republic: An American Tradition*, whiskey and cider emerged as America's most popular drinks. "Both were cheap and plentiful where available, and because they were processed in the United States from home-grown products, both benefited from nationalistic sentiment."

Also, whiskey and cider contained more alcohol than beer, which at 1 to 3 percent ABV (alcohol by volume) was considered too weak for American tastes. When colonialists drank wine, they tended to choose highly alcoholic varieties, often fortified with distilled spirits and seldom below 20 percent alcohol. "One can only conclude that at the root of the alcoholic republic was the fact that Americans chose the most highly alcoholic beverages that they could obtain easily and cheaply," Rorabaugh surmises.[10]

In *A Short History of Drunkenness*, Mark Forsyth chronicles how a taste for spirits, and whiskey in particular, was largely the result of the great push westward that began in the mid-nineteenth century. "There is one problem with beer and that problem is transport. A barrel of beer is a heavy thing and compared to a barrel of spirits, it doesn't contain very much alcohol. If you are a settler heading west into the great unknown, with limited space and weight in your wagon train, a barrel of whiskey will get you a lot drunker and a lot farther."[11]

Many of the settlers hailed from a variety of European backgrounds, such as German, Scottish and Irish, that had strong legacies of distilling fruit brandies or grain spirits. The frontier proved to be an ideal place for distilling whiskey, with plentiful water, ample fields for growing grain and bountiful wood to heat the stills.

Yet whiskey barrels are not included among the detailed lists prepared by *The Prairie and Overland Traveler*, a travel guide geared toward those emigrants,

THE FIRST ARRIVAL.

Woodcut from Mark Twain's *Life on the Mississippi. Courtesy of "Documenting the American South," Libraries of the University of North Carolina, Chapel Hill.*

traders, travelers, hunters or soldiers heading out to this new frontier. While this guide takes great care in describing proper packing and transporting procedures for a range of provisions from bacon to butter, the only drink this guide mentions by name is coffee.[12]

In his seminal work *Life on the Mississippi*, humorist and Old Crow aficionado[13] Mark Twain offers this succinct account of how whiskey won the West.

> *How solemn and beautiful is the thought that the earliest pioneer of civilization, the van-leader of civilization, is never the steamboat, never the railroad, never the newspaper, never the Sabbath school, never the missionary—but always whiskey! Such is the case. Look history over; you will see. The missionary comes after the whiskey. I mean he arrives after the whiskey has arrived; next comes the poor immigrant, with axe and hoe and rifle; next, the trader; next, the miscellaneous rush; next, the gambler, the desperado, the highwayman and all their kindred in the sin of both sexes; and next, the smart chap who has bought up an old grant that covers all the land; this brings the lawyer tribe; the vigilance committee brings the undertaker. All these interests bring the newspaper; the newspaper starts up politics and a railroad; all hands turn to and build a church and a jail—*

and behold, civilization is established forever in the land. But whiskey, you see, was the vanleader in this beneficent work. It always is. It was like a foreigner—and excusable in a foreigner—to be ignorant of this great truth, and wander off into astronomy to borrow a symbol. But if he had been conversant with the facts, he would have said, Westward the Jug of Empire takes its way.[14]

This spirited westward expansion continues to this day, with Washington State now ranking as one of the top states in terms of the total number of operating craft distilleries, though it ranks only no. 36 in terms of alcohol consumption with 2.25 gallons consumed per capita.[15] (In comparison, New Hampshire was listed as no. 1 at 4.83 gallons per capita as of 2020.)[16] The latter statistic seems to point toward a preference among Washington State residents for quality over quantity when it comes to their liquor. Yet no book exists to date that speaks to the history of the role distillers played in shaping what has grown into a multimillion-dollar industry with over one hundred active distillery licenses issued by the Washington State Liquor and Cannabis Board (LCB).

Throughout this book, I will trace the history of the barrel and the bottle from the earliest settler times to the current craft distilling boom. While the Oregon Territory, approved by Congress on August 14, 1848, initially included the states of Oregon, Washington, Idaho and parts of Montana and Wyoming, this book will focus on the history of distilled spirits in the geographical region that became Washington State in 1889.[17]

In *Scoundrels and Saloons*, Rick Mole documents how the issues surrounding the availability of liquor and the monetary profit from it link past and present like nothing else. "Liquor defeated many provincial and state politicians but elected others; it pitted small-town folk against big-city residents, gentiles against Jews, Catholics against Protestants and evangelicals against everyone else. It clogged the courts, filled the jails, plunged thousands of families into poverty and destroyed the self-esteem, careers and lives of countless individuals."[18]

So grab a glass of your favorite Pacific Northwest spirit, sit back and take a sip. Meet the legends, the bootleggers and the outliers responsible for the liquor you're holding in your hand. Learn how the illicit and unsavory business of booze became a semirespectable craft industry in Washington State. Now drink in and savor the stories (some of which are true).

Chapter 1

HOW WHISKEY WON
THE PACIFIC NORTHWEST

As Dane Huckelbridge, author of *Bourbon: A History of the American Spirit*, observes, "Whiskey and the West have been on intimate terms since our nation's first teetering baby steps in cowboy boots. Any fur trapper, prospector or horse trader who alighted upon lands wild and unknown was almost certain to have some whiskey on his person for the dual purposes of consumption and commerce."

Huckelbridge adds, "Pacific Northwest lore and legend begin with the adventures of Lewis and Clark circa 1804, though history books tend to leave out the six kegs of whiskey they brought on their journey. Nor do they elaborate on the struggles they had when they ran out of the hard stuff at the Great Falls and how the journey that followed proved challenging without it."[19]

But these men were not the first white men to set foot in this land. These pioneers followed paths originally set by American fur traders. As documented by author Susan Cheever in her book *Drinking in America: Our Secret History*, these solitary souls lived off the grid but would congregate for an annual monthlong drunken blowout called the rendezvous.

These commercial and social gatherings, first held at Henry's Fork on the Green River, were arranged by eastern fur companies to centralize the trade of furs. Men who lived and hunted alone for eleven months were thrown together with the money, whiskey and tobacco they received for the furs they trapped during the year—there was little stable currency west of the Mississippi. Over time, the rendezvous grew into a great Rocky Mountain

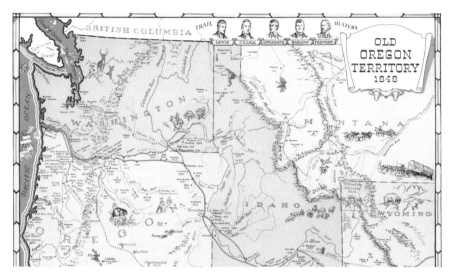

Map of the Old Oregon Territory, 1846. *Public domain.*

gathering, combining aspects of a carnival, a souk, a showdown and a rodeo. The proceedings reached their climax when the whiskey kegs were de-bunged and a saloon was improvised under a tent.[20]

Huckelbridge notes how, with stagecoaches and railroads still in the offing, the first whiskey to hit the frontier was more often than not rotgut (so named for its effect on the drinker's internal organs),[21] and for a pretty good reason—neither the mountain men nor the Native Americans for whom it was intended were in a very good position to negotiate its quality or demand otherwise.

A frontier traveler by the name of Irwin S. Cobb described the murky "corn licker" he sampled as follows, "It smells like gangrene starting in a mildewed silo, it tastes like the wrath to come and when you absorb a deep swig of it you have all the sensations of having swallowed a lighted kerosene lamp." The names used to describe western whiskey included *tanglefoot, skull varnish, tarantula juice, bug juice* and *snake water.*

The liquor used to barter with the Natives was even more toxic, as indicated in this recipe provided by frontiersman "Teddy Blue" Abbott.

> *You take one barrel of Missouri River water and two gallons of alcohol. Then you add two ounces of strychnine to make them crazy—because strychnine is the greatest stimulant in the world—and three plugs of tobacco to make them sick—an Indian wouldn't figure it was whisky unless it made*

him sick—and five bars of soap to give it a bead and half a pound of red pepper, and then you put in some sagebrush and boil it until it's brown. Strain into a barrel, and you've got your Indian whisky; that one bottle calls for one buffalo robe and when the Indian got drunk it was two robes. And that's how some of the traders made their fortune.

In addition to new diseases, decimated game stocks and befouled water sources, local tribes had to contend with the grip of the white man's "firewater." Laws against selling liquor to the Natives went back as far as 1802, but given the potential profits involved, such prohibitions were roundly ignored.[22] (Side note: Native testimony before a U.S. court of law was not recognized as that of a human being until 1847. They weren't granted citizenship until 1924, and their right to vote was not secured nationwide until 1962.)[23] Along those lines, a law passed in 1859 made it a crime to sell to the Kanakas, or Hawaiian Islanders).[24]

Origins of Distilling in the Oregon Territory

Back in 1811, John Jacob Astor's Pacific Fur Company established a permanent presence at Fort Astoria in Oregon. After a series of transactions, the British-based Hudson Bay Company (HBC) acquired this property. When the regional manager of the HBC visited this site in 1824, he deemed it inadequate. So he ordered a new fort constructed upriver named Fort Vancouver, with Dr. John McLoughlin placed in charge.

The HBC sought to create a self-sufficient community with McLoughlin overseeing the planting of wheat, vegetables and fruit trees, along with grapevines using seeds brought from England in 1825.[25] The following year, an experimental crop of barley far exceeded expectations and they began brewing beer. In 1829, one of McLoughlin's lieutenants visited Hawaii and announced that the HBC would soon be exporting beer and surplus agricultural production to the islands, with the HBC importing sugar, molasses and guest workers.

In 1833, the HBC constructed a distillery in the village of Vancouver. While the actual remains of this distillery were never found, its location is estimated to have been on the Columbia River near Joe's Crab Shack. No records exist detailing the spirits made, though available raw materials included fruit for brandy, Hawaiian molasses for rum and grain for whiskey.

A barrel/keg tap (FOVA 15696) and spigot (FOVA 268). *Courtesy of Fort Vancouver National Historic Site (U.S. National Park Service).*

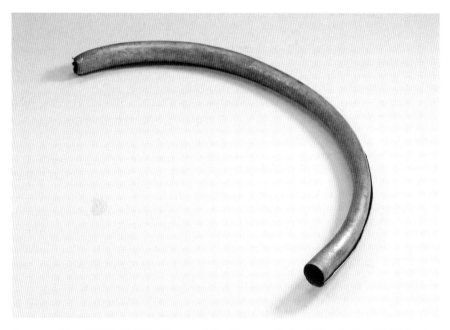

Copper tubing (FOVA 15436). *Courtesy of Fort Vancouver National Historic Site (U.S. National Park Service).*

In addition, beer/keg spigots and a copper tube discovered during the archaeological evacuation in the village area could be from either the HBC distillery or the villagers' attempts at home distilling.[26] HBC imported but strictly regulated the distribution of beer, wine and distilled spirits at Fort Vancouver, although the black market trade of local "country-made" whiskey continued. Liquor bottles, decanters and beer steins found during this evacuation point to ample drinking throughout the village.

After three years, HBC's distillery ceased operations due to what McLoughlin deemed "the bad effect it had on our affairs," adding he "would recommend, if possible, never to attempt it again." Given the long-standing tradition of trading liquor for goods with the native tribes, one can assume local Chinook leaders expressed concern about the intoxicating effects liquor had on their members. Since the HBC needed to maintain a cordial relationship with the natives so they could conduct their profitable fur trade, McLoughlin opted to close down the distillery.[27]

LIQUOR AND THE LAW

Shortly after the establishment of Fort Vancouver, parties of white missionaries and settlers began arriving in search of souls and saloons, respectively. Not surprisingly, the freedom-loving settlers resented the oppressive dictates of Christian reformers such as Dr. Elijah White, a former New York State physician who set about confiscating liquor. This zealot provoked the ire of both missionaries and settlers by calling himself "governor" and "U.S. sub-Indian agent." It was a laughable boast because the United States had no jurisdiction over the territory.[28]

Meanwhile, James Conner, an ex-HBC employee, began operating a still near Oregon City, producing a concoction popularly known as "Blue Ruin" made from Hawaiian molasses with wheat and shorts thrown in for flavoring (shorts being a byproduct of flour production, consisting mostly of the fragmented outer husk of the wheat kernel). It was marketed to the residents of Fort Vancouver and local tribes as whiskey but was actually wheat-flavored rum because the absence of malt in the mash meant none of the wheat's starch could be converted to sugar. Conner and his crew encountered the wrath of White, who with ten "noble volunteers," smashed their still, bottles and jugs. Enraged, Conner challenged White to a duel. Given that dueling was deemed illegal in the Oregon Territory, White promptly reported Conner to local authorities. Conner was arrested, fined $500 and disenfranchised for life.[29]

By 1843, anxious settlers met to form a provisional government to focus on the proliferation of makeshift illicit stills that sometimes produced "firewater" so volatile it burst into flames. As the proposed bill's preamble states, wilderness legislators feared that distilling or selling "ardent spirits" would invite "swarms of the dissipated inhabitants of other countries" and "bring upon us the swarms of savages now in our midst." Given the settlers' anxieties, this prohibition law passed easily.

For white settlers, there was still no law against having a drink, but liquor traffic was abolished. Fines included fifty dollars for those caught importing booze with the intent to sell, twenty dollars for its sale and one hundred dollars for its manufacture. But within a year, Fort Vancouver's clerks were again pouring liquor. Those desiring reform shifted from prohibiting the manufacture or sale of liquor to white settlers toward regulating distilled spirits.

In 1849, legislators in the Oregon Territory passed a licensing act that forbade the sale or gift of alcohol to Indians but established a liberal policy toward saloon licensure. Subsequent efforts to outlaw the sale and manufacture of liquor to white settlers failed to pass throughout the nineteenth century. Laws prohibited southern slaves and Natives' use of liquor even though the percentage of white heavy drinkers in any town or city likely far exceeded the same percentage found on most Native reserves.[30]

WESTWARD EXPANSION

Hollywood likes to portray the Wild West as a world of relative paupers, a land of poor but dishonest men who occasionally had to endure a moneyed interloper from the East Coast. But as Forsyth points out, the reverse is true. "People didn't go west to become poor; that would be silly. They went west because wages out there were roughly double what they were on the East Coast. There would be booms—mining booms, fur booms, cattle booms—and there wouldn't be nearly enough labor to supply the market. So wages shot up, while the overpopulated East Coast went hungry."[31]

Those pioneers venturing to the Pacific Northwest first settled along the Columbia River, beginning near the Walla Walla area, a valuable trade center for the HBC. Expansion came to a temporary halt in 1847 due to disputes with the local tribes following the Whitman Massacre. Money-eyed

Photograph of a tent saloon taken in the Yukon Territory of the type erected by the first settlers to the Oregon Territory. *Courtesy of Klondike Gold Rush National Historical Park–Seattle Unit, Clark Kinsey Collection.*

missionaries garnered cash and congregants by elevating missionary Marcus Whitman and his wife to the status of Christian martyrs murdered for their faith by savages. (Blaine Harden debunks this misguided missional myth in his book *Murder at the Mission*.) During this fighting, many people remained in this area and were on friendly terms with the local tribes, but little new settlement was allowed until 1859, when this area was reopened.[32]

The discovery of gold at Sutter's Creek in California in July 1848 enticed settlers to venture further south and west. Settlers moved to the Willamette Valley and, finally, to the river basins south of Puget Sound and on Puget Sound. To give an idea of the extent of this expansion, in 1850, there were only 62 farms north of the Columbia River, with almost all located in the valleys south of Puget Sound or near Fort Vancouver. By 1860, there were 330 farms, with the vast majority located in western Washington.[33]

The downside was that infrastructure didn't follow fast enough. There were no roads or railways, no courthouses or sheriffs, and there were no bars.[34] Until a proper saloon could be erected, a tent similar to the ones set

Jewett's saloon (Ellensburg), circa 1880s. John W. Jewett built the first saloon, which was the third business in town. The saloon was located on the south side of Third Avenue between Main and Water Streets. Settlers and townsmen were always welcomed; transient bad men and gamblers were not. By 1887, Jewett had sold most of his property, and he eventually settled in Okanogan County, where he died in 1903. *Courtesy of Ellensburg Public Library.*

up for the rendezvous would often suffice as the local drinking hole. More permanent watering holes were usually built before other establishments.[35] Especially popular in early mining camps, the saloon functioned as a poor man's club and community social center. There were often no restrictions on the vending of liquor, and whiskey was the favorite drink, taken straight and at a gulp.[36]

For those who consider saloons emblematic icons of the Wild West, it was common in the mid-nineteenth century for men throughout the United States to drink repeatedly, morning, noon and night, on an almost daily basis. While one could purchase liquor from the local merchant while shopping for other necessities or obtain a prescription for medicinal whiskey, most drinking was done in saloons. Many saloons established no age limit; young teenagers dropped in for a quick one on the way home from school or after work in the forests or fields.

Between 1880 and 1890, Portland, the Dalles and Walla Walla continued to play important roles as jumping-off points as the population of the state grew by 380 percent. But with the Northern Pacific Railway bypassing Walla Walla and building a spur from Spokane through Lewiston–Clarkston Valley

Warwick Saloon (109 West Fourth Avenue, Ellensburg), circa 1900–1909. This saloon, owned and operated by Sam Pearson, was located in the southern part of the Cadwell-Olympia Building. This was one of the most popular saloons in the area, principally with the old-timers. It carried large stocks of the best on the market in the line of wines, whiskeys and cigars. *Courtesy of Ellensburg Public Library.*

(LC Valley to the north), new cities were fast developing this role: Seattle and Tacoma on Puget Sound, LC Valley in the east and Yakima in the center of the region. Despite the Great Fire of 1889 that decimated much of Seattle, the city became the new gold crossroads, causing a flurry of economic activity unmatched in the city's history.

This westward migration was further fueled by the Klondike phenomenon in 1897. Seattle-based outfitters such as the Seattle Clothing Co. and Palmer Bros. might not have included alcohol in their extensive lists of supplies needed to outfit a man for a year,[37] though as indicated by the brisk business done by saloons, whiskey clearly continued to be a major player as prospectors ventured north.

Washington State was the place to be. If you couldn't find gold in the hills of the north country, you could make gold selling hope to fools. Likewise, if you couldn't realize money as a farmer, you could sell the promise of wealth. It was an era rich in schemes.[38]

Top: Casassa's Saloon (Ronald), circa 1900–1909. Peter Casassa (1871–1937), an Italian immigrant, arrived in Roslyn in 1892 to work in the coal mines. Later, he operated saloons in Roslyn and Ronald. *Courtesy of Ellensburg Public Library.*

Bottom: Olympia Bar (10111 Main Street, Bothell), date unknown. From the beginnings of Bothell, there has always been a tavern at this location. *Courtesy of Bothell Historical Museum.*

Independent Saloon (Cle Elum), 1910. Several men in this photograph have been superimposed, resulting in what appear to be saloon ghosts of the past. This could be an example of "compositing" by way of layering negatives or a result of partial exposures. The saloon was located between the Red Front Livery Stables and the First National Bank. *Courtesy of Ellensburg Public Library.*

These shenanigans included passing off lousy swill as legitimate spirits. In the days before distillers created trademarked brands and custom-shaped bottles with labels, they sold barrels to rectifiers, which included wholesalers, grocers and saloon owners. The more reputable establishments stocked fine wine, liquor and cigars from well-established importers based in San Francisco, Portland and Seattle. Also, genuine aged whiskey was preferred for medicinal use.

Less savory sorts would access books like *The Manufacture of Liquors, Wines, and Cordials Without the Aid of Distillation* by Pierre Lacour (1853) and *The Bar-Tender's Guide* (1862) that taught the art of faking spirits like whiskey, gin, genever, brandy and absinthe.[39] As reported by the *Mason County Journal* in 1894, some imitations were made from cheap and vile potato spirit, flavored with various oils, and toned up by such deadly poisons as sulfate of copper, chloroform and sulfuric acid. In this newspaper's analysis,

Many who imagine that they are consuming the distilled essence of corn and rye may be surprised to learn that there is very little genuine liquor in the

Right: First Avenue Saloon (Seattle), 1914. *Courtesy of the Seattle Municipal Archives.*

Below: Club Saloon (Lowell), 1891. *Courtesy of Everett Public Library.*

market. It does not pay to sell it when imitations can be made at a cost of one dollar a gallon. Also, ordinary wines, though less injurious, are equally fraudulent, consisting largely of seasoned cider, boracic, log weed and various coloring matters. Even beer is not above suspicion, malt and hops are being replaced by various chemicals, to secure larger profits. Perhaps it would be best to avoid all these drinks. Verily there is death in the cup.[40]

WHAT THE HECK IS HOOCH?

Those prospectors unable to purchase alcohol from legitimate importers or more unsavory channels could avail themselves of a devilish concoction called *hoochinoo*, from which we get the slang term *hooch* to describe an illicitly distilled and typically inferior liquor. With the U.S. purchase of the Alaskan territory in 1867, soldiers were dispatched to out-of-the-way outposts in the Alaskan wilderness where there was no easy access to alcohol. Apparently, a group of soldiers stationed on Admiralty Island near Juneau began to brew an extremely potent spirit out of molasses, yeast, berries, sugar and graham flour. This liquor became a trade item between the soldiers and a nearby Indian tribe, the Hutsnuwu (Hoochinoo). This local tribe subsequently learned how to make hoochinoo and began trading this new spirit with their neighbors. According to another rumor, the Hutsnuwu tribe learned how to distill from American fur traders.[41] What can be agreed on is that this concoction could kill. (Other names used to describe illegally distilled spirits included *moonshine*—so named as it was distilled under moonlight to avoid being detected—*mountain dew* and *catdaddy*.)[42]

According to multiple newspaper accounts, those selling liquor to the natives would be prosecuted if caught. On November 15, 1891, the *Seattle Post-Intelligencer* reported the first account of such an arrest, where five half-breed moonshiners were arrested in West Seattle for conducting an illicit distillery in the brush and selling liquor to Indians.

PIONEERING ATTEMPTS AT COMMERCIAL DISTILLING

After HBC's distillery closed in 1836, the next documented reference to a Washington State–based distillery can be found in Martin Sobmier's obituary. Sobmier came to Steilacoom, where he started a brewery and distillery in 1859 before moving to Seattle in 1863, where he established the North Pacific Brewery.[43]

According to the *Spokesman-Review*, in 1862, Major Curtis from Fort Colville went to the distillery in Pinkney City, which was the county seat of Spokane County at this time. "He took the worm of the still out and up to the fort, knocked all the barrels of whisky in the head and ordered everyone in town not to sell liquor to anyone, which order was obeyed, not only because it was an order but for self-protection."[44]

Two years later, A. Rose & Co. erected a distillery near Meyer's Brewery at the east end of Walla Walla. A year later, the paper reported the mill and distillery would be in running order in ninety days.

Then in 1867, reports surfaced that a new liquor distillery under construction for the firm of Overholtzer & Scott at their gristmill on Yellow Hawk Creek would be completed and in running order by next spring.[45] According to bankruptcy papers filed in 1870, Overholtzer & Scott's business included 140 acres with a gristmill and distillery. They went to J.C. Smith

LaFortune's Eureka Saloon (222 Main Street, Walla Walla), circa 1903. *Courtesy of Bygone Walla Walla (wallawalladrazanphotos.blogspot.com).*

and asked to borrow some money to pay off their debt. J.C. Smith agreed to lend the money at a 2% rate and included three hundred bushels of wheat in this loan. When Samuel Jacobs threatened the business with a lawsuit for the $300 owed him, they allegedly transferred or sold 9,500 gallons of distilled spirits, the land, the mill and the distillery to a third party to hold for them while the business declared bankruptcy.[46] The Overholtzer and Scott families left Washington State after this incident.

By 1877, the Washington Territory could claim fourteen breweries but no fruit or grain distilleries, though this absence wasn't due to an ongoing lack of trying.[47]

A year after the Washington Territory became Washington State in 1889, Centralia received an offer from a Kentucky distillery to put up a plant in that burg if a bonus could be raised for it.[48] Also in Wenatchee, Shotwell & Miller started their distillery to work up the fruit that could not be sold.[49] In 1893, Spokane Distilling planned to locate in Trent, thus making it a suburb of Spokane. The distillery would start with only sixty bushels a day, but the capacity was expected to increase with the growth of the business.[50]

By 1894, there were 1,930 breweries and 4,791 distilleries in the United States.[51] On paper, this year looked to be a boom year for projected distilleries in Washington State. In Goldendale, G.B. Goodell, president of the Distilling Company at Grant's, said the distillery would be in operation as soon as the necessary repairs could be made. In addition, a distillery to make alcohol from wood was being projected by eastern parties in Aberdeen.[52]

In addition, a Spokane distillery had been sold by the sheriff for $26,000. One could presume this was Spokane Distilling, though the exact name of this particular distillery is not listed. Also, George C. Bott, proprietor of the Monogram saloon, was working up a scheme to establish a $1,000,000 distillery east of the mountains. He figured on using 80 percent rye, 10 percent corn and 10 percent malt in the manufacture of the very finest rye whiskey. He had made a proposition to the Selah Valley Ditch Company to locate a distillery and raise barley and rye extensively.[53] Also, a syndicate of Tacoma and eastern capitalists was building a big distillery and securing three thousand acres of land under the Selah Valley Ditch on which to grow rye and barley.[54]

The following year, the *Dawn* reported on Philip Miller's success in the brandy business over in Wenatchee: "Four years ago, I put in a small copper distillery. I make about 500 gallons of brandy a year, and which I sell at $5 per gallon. My brandies are equal to the old Kentucky brandies and are pronounced the best that can be had in this country."[55]

Holland Gin label for medicinal liquor dispensed by the Stuart & Holmes Drug Company (Walla Walla). *Courtesy of Bygone Walla Walla (wallawalladrazanphotos.blogspot.com).*

Even though Oregon had a much smaller population than Washington, it loomed up grandly in the liquor census, using eight times as much distilled spirits as Washington in the "arts, manufactures and medicine," which means drugstore trade. Throughout Oregon, medicine stores sold 15,237 gallons of whiskey and brandy in 1889; those in Washington sold 4,529.[56] Simply put, in Washington State, the saloons were patronized; in Oregon, the apothecary shops. While no reason was given for this particular trend, prescribing whiskey and other distilled spirits to treat a range of ailments was common practice during this time.

In 1889, the *Spokane Falls Review* referenced a licensed distillery that had been in operation for six months, though the name of the distillery is not mentioned.[57] This same year, the *Pullman Herald* reported that "the Uniontown Distillery has been organized, and we expect to give our readers the news that the institution is in full running order." The following year, this paper noted that the Uniontown Distillery was now defunct.[58]

In Walla Walla distilling news, Edward Cochran of Waitsburg was working to move his distillery from its current (undisclosed) location to Walla Walla circa 1900.[59] Also, as reported by the *Seattle Post-Intelligencer*, Theyss and J.W. Medynski of La Salle were in Walla Walla looking over the ground for the erection of a distillery. The chief difficulty was the matter of freights and the high price of coal. They were corresponding with the railway companies, and if satisfactory arrangements could be made, there was a probability that the works would be erected. Should that be the case, they would be of great benefit to farmers and would open up a profitable local market for large quantities of corn and rye, which grew to perfection there.[60] Pre-pro.com, a website serving as a repository for information about the pre-Prohibition liquor industry, lists two transactions recorded in 1903 and 1904 for two warehouses located in or near Walla Walla that were carried out by Walla Walla Distillery and Thos Segraves, respectively. During this time, two transactions were recorded for a warehouse located in or near Davenport that were carried out by Chas Goans, and a transaction was recorded in 1904 for a warehouse located in or near Vancouver that was carried out by White Bros.[61]

As per the *Seattle Star*, "A BIG distillery is planned at Sedro-Woolley in 1905." The following year, this paper reported that "many of the people of Green Lake are very indignant over the fact that Sol Levinson, the liquor dealer, is trying to get a permit to build a blackberry brandy distillery here.[62]

In 1907, a whiskey distillery with a capacity of one thousand barrels annually was slated to be erected in Everett by a firm run out of North Carolina.[63] Also in 1907, Kirkwood Distillery Company and Fox River Distillery Company were listed by the *Yakima Herald* in its report on a dispute over the sale of the Rainer Saloon.[64]

Even though none of these distilleries appeared to be sustainable businesses, the liquor industry was booming in Washington State, especially in Seattle. According to Keith Barnes, president and cofounder of Motive Marketing Group Inc. and founder of Bainbridge Organic Distillers, around this time, 111 Yesler (the site where Pioneer Square sits today) was the location of the bar alternately known as La Boheme and the Bohemian Liquor House. The production of liquor on the site of a commercial bar was not that unusual before Prohibition, with 137 Seattle-based distillers and wholesalers making a living from the liquor industry from 1870 to 1920. To put this number into proper perspective, over twenty-four thousand individuals were working in the liquor trade throughout the United States during this same time.[65]

Unlike many similar operations, the Bohemian Liquor Company went the extra mile by getting a license from the federal government to distill and distribute liquor in 1911 and 1912. D.R. (Dave) Himelhoch was the owner/operator of the distillery side of the Bohemian enterprise and had another distilling operation a few blocks away at 810 Main Street in Seattle. The location of this distillery would not be thought of as respectable for another seventy years. The Bohemian Liquor House was shuttered by Prohibition, and little can be found as to the fortunes of Mr. Himelhoch.

After the end of prohibition, 111 Yesler was back in business as a bar under the name Sully's Snow Goose. By 1956, the location was once again pouring under the nameplate of the Bohemian Tavern. In 1960, it became the Totem Pole Tavern, likely taking advantage of the new totem pole erected at Pioneer Square in 1940 after the original totem pole (stolen from a Tlingit Indian village in Alaska by a group of wealthy Seattleite "expeditioners" forty-one years prior) was destroyed by an arson fire. This address changed to One Eleven Yesler Tavern in 1965, and then from the early 1970s to 1992, it was the Pioneer Square Tavern, until it became the first home of the Fenix Cafe. Remodeling made room for additional bars, including a new Bohemian (Club), Velvet Elvis and Trinity. In 2005, Bohemian Club became Formosa Card Room, and Trinity Night Club still occupies the space.[66]

The *1914 Yakima County & North Yakima Buyers Guide* included the Yakima Distilling Company, distillers of pure fruit brandies, with Thomas Kennerly as president and treasurer. Kennerly is listed in the 1913 edition as a distiller, but there is no mention of this distillery or Kennerly in the 1915 edition.[67]

The inability of any distillery to garner a strong foothold in Washington State at this juncture points to the complications of launching a business during this period of encroaching governmental oversight. State and local municipalities continued to vote for laws outlawing liquor and raising liquor taxes. Now add in the difficulties of trying to run a legitimate business when one has to compete with an overabundance of unregulated whiskey produced by illicit distillers, wholesalers, saloon owners, rectifiers and the like, all of whom sold products that were liable to be unsavory at best but usually cost less than commercially produced spirits.

THE RISE OF ILLICIT DISTILLING

After the Whiskey Rebellion of 1794, which arose following the federal government's decision to tax American-made whiskey, the U.S. government left distillers alone until the War of 1812, when a federal tax was imposed briefly on distilled spirits as a way to finance the war.[68] This tax imposed on both beer and whiskey to help fund the Civil War led to an outbreak of illicit distilling.[69] Jacob M. Woodring, a blacksmith of Mount Vernon, had the distinction of being the first moonshiner brought before the federal court in Seattle, in 1899.[70]

Otto Peterson, the proprietor of the only store in Marblemount, recounts how he sold operators (a.k.a. moonshiners) "tons of sugar, corn meal, rye meal and charred oak barrels." His clients were primarily loggers from North Carolina who came to the Upper Skagit in the early 1900s and brought with

Violin performance in saloon (Port Angeles). Two men are playing violins in an unidentified saloon. George Parks is on the left. The other two men in this photo are not identified.
Courtesy of Kellogg Collection of the North Olympic Library System.

them the pioneer southern tradition of making, drinking and marketing corn whiskey. He said bootleggers paid twelve dollars a gallon, divided it into twelve "short pints" instead of eight 16-ounce pints, and resold it for two dollars per short pint, a 100 percent profit. The distribution system was simple and efficient: the moonshiners would bring it to a "cache," a hiding place near town, possibly behind a blackberry bush. The bootlegger would pay the middleman and then be directed to where the liquor was stashed. Of course, no state or federal taxes were paid.[71]

These illegal actions weren't confined to rural areas or the South. City people were making whiskey, and it was in cities and immigrant neighborhoods where law enforcement agents focused the bulk of their efforts. To give one an idea of the scope of distillers operating without a license, the 1879 Internal Revenue Commissioner's report showed that over a three-year period, government agents seized 3,117 illicit distilleries and arrested 6,431 distillers, with 26 revenue agents killed and 47 wounded.[72] No accounting was given for the number of distillers killed and wounded. Given the limited coverage of distillery raids in Washington State newspapers, one can surmise that most of these seizures and arrests occurred outside the state.

SELLING SAFE SPIRITS

Three sets of legislation attempted to clean up the mess of adulterated and falsely advertised whiskey in America: the Bottled-in-Bond Act of 1897, which created a certification for unadulterated whiskey and now includes all spirits; the Pure Food and Drug Act of 1906, which prohibited "adulterated or misbranded or poisonous or deleterious liquors, foods, drugs or medicines"; and the Taft Decision of 1909, which finally created definitions for bourbon and other whiskeys produced in the United States.[73] As liquor laws tightened, those farmers who sold their harvest to distilleries were given the option by the government to dispose of their wares at a fair price. Their goods would be used to make industrial (ethyl) alcohol used for fuel, lighting and heating purposes. This denatured alcohol is free from taxes but rendered unfit for use as a beverage by mixing it with wood (methyl) alcohol, a harmful liquid that could cause blindness or death if ingested.[74]

Yet, as we shall see in the next chapter, the distilling, distribution and consumption of unlicensed liquor remained a constant concern at the start of the twentieth century. So replenish your drink, though bear in mind that when consuming late nineteenth and early twentieth-century spirits, it's best to stick to those spirits that were bottled-in-bond or distilled by a trusted source.

Saloon in Everett during pre-Prohibition times. *Courtesy of Everett Public Library.*

Chapter 2

THE RIGHTEOUS WAR
AGAINST ALCOHOL

There was a popular perception throughout the West, recounted by Forsyth, that husbands would get paid, go to the saloon, spend all their wages and return home penniless and angry, where they would beat their wives. The wives lived in bruised poverty because the saloons took all the money. Nobody knows to what extent this is true. Domestic violence is a notoriously difficult crime to get figures on while it's happening, and what precisely occurred in what percentage of log cabins is something that we shall never reconstruct.[75]

While we can't prove definitively what happened when the men returned home, saloons throughout the United States encouraged a scale of drunkenness unimaginable today. Even the Yakima Indians pleaded with the government to keep saloons off their reservation.[76]

To give an idea of the number of saloons in Washington State, according to the Ferry County Historical Society, one of their informants, no longer available for comment, told them there were fourteen saloons in Republic in his young days before World War I. He and his brothers tried to have a drink in all of them on payday evenings but never made it to all of them. The saloon farthest north on the way out of town had a sign with different messages on its two sides: "Last Chance" on the northbound side and "First Chance" on the southbound. In 1910, the population of Republic was under one thousand but well over five hundred.[77]

Similar numbers could be found in towns throughout the state. There were more saloons than ever before, more rowdy patrons, more violent behavior

Baker's Saloon, a.k.a. Pend Oreille Tavern (Metaline Falls), circa 1905–10. Art Baker is the bartender. *Courtesy of Pend Oreille County Library District.*

and arrests for drunkenness and more suffering families.[78] In the Pacific Northwest, Protestants, Catholics and Jews in the late nineteenth century found themselves virtually overwhelmed by an emerging urban culture based primarily on alcohol consumption, gambling, prostitution and other inexpensive recreational activities ranging from unregulated theaters and movies to dance halls, race tracks and amusement parks.[79] A 1894 ban on liquor sales in box houses in Seattle failed to stem the tide of liquor flowing throughout the city. Ships coming into Seattle were always loaded with plenty of gold and men. Mayor Tom Humes, who recognized the benefits of both the ladies and Seattle's legitimate businesses, allowed the town to remain "wide open."[80]

Such concerns for public safety were not unfounded. Take the single saloon in Kiona that became the nightly destination of over four hundred railroad workers. If they ventured near the raucous site, wide-eyed residents could watch the barkeeps literally throwing the semicomatose drunks out the back door, where they landed, retching and shaking, in a tangle of arms and legs.[81]

In response to such flagrant displays of public drunkenness, state legislators voted on November 14, 1879, to prohibit the sale of liquor within a mile of the Northern Pacific Railroad during its construction in Spokane, Stevens and Whitman Counties. Laws like this failed to stem the tide of dangerous, and at times deadly, actions stemming from the saloon culture. For instance, by the early 1900s, Aberdeen was thought to be "the roughest town west of the Mississippi" because of excessive gambling, violence and drug use. This old logging city was even off-limits to military personnel until the late 1950s.[82]

Despite the saloon's violent history, Hollywood depictions of cowboys or cowhands offering the bartender a .45-caliber rifle cartridge in exchange for a shot of whiskey are more legendary than logical. The term *shot of whiskey* didn't become commonplace until the mid-twentieth century, and a shot of whiskey would have cost ten .45-caliber rifle cartridges.[83]

The term Skid Road (or Skid Row) has its origins in the lumberjack camps of the Pacific Northwest dating to the earliest pioneer days, when teams of oxen and horses would haul cut timber along a road carved out of the wilderness. This road would have wooden slats greased with bacon grease or other lubricants on hand to ease the pulling of logs over them and then out to the sawmills. This practice continues to this day, though sans the bacon grease, with this practice conducted outside the city limits.

But in the nineteenth century, loggers would skid logs down the steep hills of Mill Street in Seattle (now renamed Yesler Way) leading down to Henry Yesler Mill.[84] Over time, *skid row* evolved from a neutral term describing a common logging practice to a derogatory slur directed at the rough and tough loggers who frequented "Our House," a combination saloon and bank based in Seattle, as well as the grittiest part of any city that was inhabited by gamblers, drunks and other ne'er-do-wells.[85]

As late as 1914, Seattle's *Argus* reported, "There are saloons in which fights are of a nightly occurrence…where drunks are 'rolled'…where the man who gets his check cashed stands powerful little show of getting away with any of the coin…where liquor is sold to boys."[86] According to the *Spokane Falls Review*, the saloon atmosphere consisted of floors covered with peanuts, spilt beer and tobacco smoke with a smell so bad that a monkey who escaped from an animal act and died under the floor of the Casino Theater was not discovered until a year later, when some repairs were being made.[87]

In another story recounted by Russ Pfeiffer-Hoyt, a member of the Nesset family, this large clan of Norwegian immigrant homesteaders settled along the South Fork Nooksack River at the beginning of the nineteenth century. His great-grandfather lived near Wickersham, a logging community of about four hundred men served by one hotel saloon and one hotel brothel. No longer wishing to support his daughter, he brought her to work in one of the hotels when she was fourteen. Two years later, the owner of a small logging camp felt sorry for her and asked her to work as a cook in his logging camp.[88]

Torino Saloon (Roslyn), circa 1910–19. *Courtesy of Ellensburg Public Library.*

Stories of ill treatment and illegalities within the saloon culture, especially those involving women and children, went largely unreported. This raises the question posed by Cheever, "When does drinking become more than just a little harmless enjoyment?" She notes that in history and in one's personal life, drinking has to be judged by its effects—not by the quantity imbibed or the attitudes of the surrounding culture. Also, the words *alcoholism* and *alcoholic* were not even coined until the 1840s and didn't become common until the temperance movements of the 1890s. "Before then, drunks were just drunks, and drinking too much was called by many names, most of them picturesque. According to one source, *Benjamin Franklin's Drinker's Dictionary*, some synonyms for drunk can be: afflicted, piss'd in the brook, had a thump over the head with Sampson's jawbone, cherry merry, hammer-ish, haunted with evil spirits, moon-ey'd, nimptop-sical and double-tongu'd."[89] Also, the term *blotto*, used to describe someone who was inebriated to the point of unconsciousness, didn't come into use until 1917.[90]

Regardless of what one called the hordes of men imbibing in saloons at all hours of the day and night, Mark Lawrence Schrad reminds us in *Smashing the Liquor Machine: A Global History of Prohibition* that we should not be misled by historical romanticism or falsely equate the saloons of yesteryear with the well-regulated taverns and restaurants of today. "Unlike the fictional bar featured in the TV show *Cheers*, the saloonkeeper wasn't your friend: he aimed to get as much of your money as possible through under-measuring or watering down your drinks, running up your tab or enticing you with his gaming tables and prostitutes. He'd use his clout and his fists to intimidate those who disagreed with him and give some of his ill-gotten profits to corrupt politicians to look the other way."[91] Some even went so far as to sell cheap alcohol from bottles that once contained expensive liquor. Drunkards and children were served.[92]

Though saloonkeepers tried to maintain a facade of respectability, it is not as though they kept their intentions secret. In their quest for profits, they were aided and abetted by the big breweries, which paid for most, if not all, of the saloon's furnishings, along with the cutlery, glassware and food. Often, saloons would advertise "free lunch" for their customers, knowing full well that the salty fare they served would encourage their patrons to consume even more alcohol.[93] Thus the the phrase "there's no such thing as a free lunch" was born.[94]

The Corners Saloon (Sequim). Joseph L. Keeler came to Sequim in 1903. He sawed lumber for the Hotel Sinclair, built in 1908, where the saloon was first located, as well as building a saloon at the Corners, the stoplight intersection, a small hotel and a sawmill. *Courtesy of Kellogg Collection of the North Olympic Library System.*

The commercial distilleries situated largely in the Midwest and on the East Coast played a key role in keeping their customers liquored up. "We must create the appetite for liquor in growing boys," remarked one liquor man before the Retail Liquor Dealers' Association of Ohio. "Men who drink will die… and if there is no new appetite created, our counters will be empty as well as our coffers.[95]

Not all saloon owners fit this sordid description, such as James "Jimmie" Durkin, who garnered notoriety as Spokane's legendary liquor tycoon. After noticing that bars were unwisely overpaying wagon-train companies for freight deliveries from Spokane, Durkin realized that by shipping booze in by the barrel (instead of the jug), he could cut costs by 50 percent. So he opened Colville's tenth liquor outpost with a $3,500 investment that grew within a few years to $65,000. Then he launched Durkin's Bar in Spokane, where he served fine alcoholic beverages including Dewar's Scotch, Seagram's Canadian Whisky, Old Crow and Hermitage brand Kentucky whiskeys, Spanish sherries and Ireland's beloved Bass Ale and Guinness Stout, along with quality cigars. His bar not only offered better-priced drinks to its clientele, but it also earned a reputation as a relatively

The Owl Saloon (Roslyn), circa 1900–1909, one of the area's many popular saloons. It was not uncommon to send a child to a saloon with a bucket to be filled with beer and carried home to their waiting parent. *Courtesy of Ellensburg Public Library.*

respectable joint. Also, Durkin permitted those opposing the sale of liquor to post their antiliquor posters in his saloon, a move that only served to generate even more business.[96]

Men of means could retreat to their private clubs, such as the Rainer Club in Seattle, founded in 1888, or a higher quality saloon like Jim Morrison's thriving establishment at the southeast corner of Second and University in Seattle. Here, one encountered hard-eyed men well dressed in conservative, tailored suits who were professional gamblers, serious students of cards and dice or tied in with the rackets. But at least these places had the smell of success, not squalor.

SOULS VERSUS SALOONS

One might encounter. on the side street of a corner saloon, a sign reading "Family Entrance," which meant women were welcome to sit in a back room. However, any self-respecting woman would as soon appear nude at a nunnery as cross that threshold of turpitude (unless, of course, they were there in protest).[97]

Christian leaders ranging from the traveling evangelist Billy Sunday[98] to the Seattle-based Presbyterian pastor the Reverend Mark Matthews[99] preached against the evils of liquor in Washington State. They encouraged their godly followers to not only abstain from all intoxicating liquors but also encourage others to do likewise. As per historian Norman B. Clark, "These 'radicals' at the hard core of the Washington prohibition movement were dedicated alcohol fighters, absolutely convinced of the evil of all intoxicating drinks. To these men and women, the saloon was evil institutionalized, at once a symbol and an instrument of Satan's work among God's unfortunate creatures."[100]

Here are the marching songs of determined armies. This reflects an era when the knowledge of hymns was widespread; when the parlor piano, not the pot party, was the source of an evening's merriment; and where every beau was a baritone. Who now can match lines like these?

Little Drinks of brandy,
With little Sips of gin,
Swell the mighty torrents
Of disease and sin.

Or:

Many souls are in bondage, in the land of the free,
While the serpents are hiding as thick as can be;
In the bowl they are lurking and are ready to bite,
When the last dregs are guzzled in the blackness of night.[101]

The popular media depiction of those protesting against alcohol as crazy Christians armed with hatchets proved to be more fiction than fact. For starters, as Schrad notes, "When [Carrie Nation] made national headlines for smashing saloons back in Kansas, not only were those saloons operating illegally in a dry state with the connivance of local officials, she was also usually smashing them and sending the barflies to flight at *eight o'clock in the morning.*"[102]

While the bulk of the media coverage focused on the Woman's Christian Temperance Union's (WCTU) opposition to alcohol as anathema to "Christian" values, the group's most significant legacy was its grassroots impact and profound local influence. The WCTU established public libraries in communities across the nation on the grounds that reading is a means of education that leads to self-improvement and good citizenship.

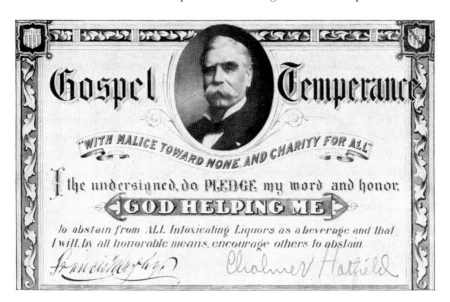

Signed Gospel Temperance Pledge. *Courtesy of Brad Holden, author of* Seattle Prohibition.

Gransch Saloon (Colton), 1917. Harry Gransch was the owner and bartender. His brother-in-law, Barney Gardewin, was also a bartender and eventually purchased the bar from Harry. *Courtesy of Whitman County Library.*

The WCTU began organizing in late 1873 in Ohio and New York, and within a year, it counted 629 members in King County alone.[103] Local units also pioneered social services to empower women, such as a children's day nursery and a women's exchange in Seattle. In Washington, the WCTU was instrumental in pushing the passage of the Alcohol Education Act in 1886 by requiring that the "effects" of alcohol and narcotics be taught in public schools. Under the law, the county treasurer was to withhold county funds from those schools that did not comply.[104]

African American women formed their own chapters of the WCTU. In Seattle, the Frances Harper Union formed in the mid-1880s. It was named after the first published African American woman novelist, an abolitionist and a former slave. The union's reach remained restricted due to opposition from the pastor of the African Methodist Episcopal Church in Seattle, who wanted the women to spend less time with the impoverished and more time raising money to pay off the church mortgage.[105] Supposedly there was an African American WCTU chapter in Tacoma, though further evidence of this chapter cannot be found as of this writing.

Also, the Anti-Saloon League (ASL) emerged during this time, with its motto, "The Saloon Must Go!" In reality, the league wanted everything to go—not just rum shops with tawdry atmospheres but all rum shops, in addition to all breweries, all distilleries, all vineyards and, as a consequence, all customers and their horrible unceasing thirsts.[106]

According to Schrad, despite vilification by historians, the ASL never opposed alcohol itself or the individual's right to drink, even actively opposing so-called bone-dry laws that would have made actual consumption of alcohol a crime.[107] Along those lines, Clark observes how there were many parts of the state's business community who held moderate positions about liquor consumption. Most simply and directly, there were those men in the restaurant business who resented the competition of saloons and whose efforts were first directed toward laws prohibiting free lunches in saloons.

Clark summarized this war against whiskey as follows:

> *The root of it all lay in the threat of alcohol to middle-class American mores. Alcohol caused an individual to lose his self-control, and loss of self-control—physical, intellectual, sexual, financial, political—was the cardinal sin. Drunkenness, prostitution, miscegenation, venereal disease, poverty, bossism—these were the darkest threats to the values through which the American middle class had established its identity. These were the challenges to what the prohibitionists liked to call "clean, wholesome manhood."*[108]

SUFFRAGETTES VERSUS SALOONS

While the motivations of those concerned about the uptick in alcohol consumption may be somewhat murky, a clear pattern emerged between the rise of the suffragette movement and the establishment of local option laws. These laws allowed residents of a town or precinct to petition for elections on the licensing of liquor sales within their community, including the option to go "dry," which meant that alcohol could not be sold or consumed in that given town or region.

As early as 1870, Seattle attempted to close the front doors of all saloons and drinking houses on Sunday via Ordinance 10, with a twenty-five-dollar fine for those caught violating the ordinance. Saloon regulation proved to be one of the toughest selling points when Seattle tried to annex smaller cities, including Ballard, South Park and West Seattle, where the Luna Park amusement area boasted the best-stocked bar on the bay. Ballard, where fishermen and shingle mill workers enjoyed their Sunday brews, voted for annexation by a narrow 122-vote margin. Georgetown, which was home to the Rainier Brewery and others, held out until 1910.[109]

By 1883, the WCTU's efforts had gained enough momentum that women won the right to vote in Washington State. On securing this right, most women both in Washington State and throughout the United States joined forces with "law and order" men to enact local options, a move that appeared to solidify their support with the male-led antiliquor (or antisaloon, at least) advocacy efforts. Women lost the right to vote in Washington State in 1889 and did not secure it permanently until 1910, when the state's male voters ratified the statewide woman suffrage amendment by a margin of almost two to one.[110] This was a decade before the Nineteenth Amendment passed, which prohibited denying the right to vote based on sex.[111]

Local Option Laws: Wets Versus Drys

The territorial supreme court outlawed local-option prohibition in 1888, although a modified version of the law was later reinstated thanks in large part to the efforts of the WCTU and the ASL. The modified version returned the power to grant or refuse applications for saloon licenses to city councils and county commissioners and gave these bodies the right to set license fees between $300 and $1,000 annually, which enriched local coffers.

Even in dry towns, pharmacies were allowed to sell alcohol for medicinal purposes. Lemon extract with a high alcohol content could be purchased in grocery stores. Some customers used it by the teaspoon to flavor cookies; others swallowed it straight from the bottle.[112]

By 1908, Seattle would boast about 100 churches and 211 saloons. Seattle's bright, shiny new prosperity came with an ugly underside of vice and corruption.[113]

By now, the conflicts between "open-town" advocates (the "wets"), who advocated for restricted and regulated drinking, gambling and prostitution, and "closed-town" anti-vice and anti-alcohol forces (the "drys") were in full swing. As an example of these conflicts, from 1906 to 1907, Kirkland residents were deeply divided over whether or not to allow the sale of liquor inside city limits. According to a longtime Kirkland resident, Jack Ferry sold liquor illegally at his grocery store despite the fact that the city was dry.

Monahan's Liquor Store and Eagle Baths (Colfax), circa 1910. Located between Barroll Hardware and the Binnard Block, this establishment housed various businesses over the years before being torn down to provide parking and drive-up window access for Farmer's State Bank. Other signs on Monahan's Liquor Store indicate that the building also housed Edward Harpole's wine and liquor store and a cafe. *Courtesy of Whitman County Library.*

Mayor A.B. Newell enforced the prohibition law, and he and his supporters ran Ferry out of town. Feelings ran so high that someone hung Ferry in effigy in front of an ice storage shed labeled "City Hall."[114]

The Washington State Legislature passed the "Sabbath Breaking" law in 1909, which prohibited most businesses from operating on Sunday. The law was commonly called the "Blue Law" and was a very broad expansion of an 1881 law that only prohibited "fighting or offering to fight, horse-racing or dancing" on Sunday.[115] While some advocated for Blue Laws on religious grounds, others viewed them as progressive measures that prohibited employers from forcing laborers to work seven days a week with no respite in sight.

This same year, 1909, marked the first time that a stronger local option law went into effect throughout the state. Under this law, voters in any town (not just incorporated communities) could petition to hold an election to decide whether to license saloons in their community. The vote for this local option law garnered enough national media attention that renowned evangelist preacher Billy Sunday came to Friday Harbor to denounce the multiple evils of liquor and the saloons that supplied it. Not coincidentally, his sermon came one day before the statewide vote. Sunday's visit to the county seat of San Juan County capped a campaign led by the WTCU and the ASL of several decades to eliminate the negative impact of the liquor trade on those who frequented Friday Harbor's three saloons, their families and even the character of the town itself.[116]

Some of the strongest local option support came from rural residents. When farmhands left for a city visit, their frustrated farmer-employers never knew if they would return or, if they did, if they would be in any condition to work. The temptations of big-city saloons threatened every farm family's future harvest and livelihood. In many farm hamlets, saloons were the most visible sign of big-city vice and corruption and, not so incidentally, what was politely referred to as the "foreign element." Immigrants stepping off trains brought their taste for vodka, wine and beer to coastal towns and cities.[117]

Of the 220 local option elections held from 1909 to 1912, 140 resulted in dry victories. By the ASL's calculations in 1912, the dry areas of the state included 42 percent of the state's population. As documented by Clark, this included the town of Bellingham along with six counties (Cowlitz, Garfield, Island, Klickitat, Mason and San Juan), and twenty-eight others were dry outside the cities and towns.[118]

With few respectable allies, the brewers, distillers, wholesalers and dealers for a time attempted to recast their own sorry image. The brewers tried to represent themselves as honorable providers of nourishing beverages for the working classes, and the distillers loudly opposed the saloon and its accompanying evils. Unfortunately, the alcohol industry in the United States was so busy fighting for tax reform, battling with the brewers and combating fraud within their own ranks that the temperance groups were able to coalesce and garner enough support to win at the ballot box.

The wets were dealt a substantial blow in 1913 with the passage of the Sixteenth Amendment, which allowed Congress to levy a federal income tax. This new tax paved the way for national Prohibition, as the federal government no longer needed the revenue streams generated by liquor taxes.[119]

After the United States declared war on the German Empire on April 6, 1917, several factors dictated the fate of the American distiller. First, prohibitionists connected the Germans to alcohol, saying that as most American brewers were German, you couldn't trust them, and thus you must support Prohibition. Also, the grains used for making whiskey were needed for the war effort for both fuel and food, with the War Trade Board ensuring that grains were used for food and for its allies. Some distilleries converted

Postcard from the Young People's Christian Temperance Union in Chicago mailed to Chas. McLeod in Tacoma. *Courtesy of Brad Holden, author of* Seattle Prohibition.

their stills to aid the government with industrial (denatured) alcohol, and the Distillers Securities Corp. formed a subsidiary called the United States Industrial Alcohol Company to facilitate the government's needs.[120]

WASHINGTON STATE GOES DRY

After prodigious ASL lobbying efforts statewide, on November 3, 1914, Washington voters approved Initiative Measure Number Three, prohibiting the manufacture and sale (although not the consumption) of liquor statewide. The popular vote was 189,840 for and 171,208 against, with urban voters in Seattle, Tacoma and Spokane voting against this measure. In comparison, neighboring Oregon went "bone dry," allowing no liquor exemptions at all.[121]

Once this law went into effect on January 1, 1916, state residents could still consume alcohol, but a legal permit was required to import it from out-of-state vendors. Quantity was limited to either half a gallon of hard liquor or a case (twenty-four bottles) of beer per month. Alcohol could also be obtained with a valid medical prescription, prompting the opening of hundreds of new pharmacies.[122] According to anecdotal accounts, the "conditions" for which alcohol was deemed medically necessary included asthma, high blood pressure, diabetes, shock, cancer, certain kinds of poisoning, insomnia and snakebites.

The 1950s soda fountain is popularly depicted as a clean, pure milkshake and hamburger counter in a Main Street family drugstore where teenagers hang out after school. That image is a far cry from the humble origins of the soda fountain as a spigot inside a druggist's shop in the first decades of the 1800s and from the dispensaries of opioids, stimulants and patent medicines they became later in the century.[123]

Seattle mayor Hiram Gill increased enforcement efforts by establishing a Dry Squad unit of the Seattle Police Department and endorsing regular raids of homes and businesses. Mayor Gill's "strong arm" tactics won some public support, but he also faced accusations of bribery and corruption leveled at members of the Dry Squad and at Gill himself, including a federal lawsuit accusing both Gill and members of the Dry Squad of colluding with bootleggers. Despite an eventual acquittal, city council members demanded additional explanations from the accused, who eventually admitted to accepting private monies to assist with a "secret investigation" against violators of the liquor laws.[124]

Two rival gangs in Seattle controlled the rising black market for alcohol. One of these crews was headed by Edward Jack Margett (sometimes spelled Marquet), a former Seattle patrolman who was otherwise known as "Pirate Jack" due to his penchant for hijacking liquor shipments and selling the stolen alcohol from his Seattle headquarters. Battling Margett for control of the local booze market was a squad of bootleggers headed by Logan and Fred Billingsley.[125] When Washington went dry in 1916, these brothers opened the Stewart Street Pharmacy to cash in on the sudden demand for medicinal liquor. Eventually, they were forced to close their pharmacy after receiving too many citations for various liquor violations. Undeterred, the Billingsleys set up a large-scale moonshining operation in a warehouse on Seattle's Westlake Avenue and began manufacturing booze.

In response, Margett began hijacking deliveries of the Billingsleys' liquor, which set up a tense standoff between the two groups. After one intense night of gunfire, the Billingsleys hired an armed security guard to keep watch over their warehouse. On the night of July 24, 1916, two Seattle police officers were out patrolling their beat when the Billingsleys' watchmen mistook them for Margett's men and opened fire, resulting in a shootout that left the officers dead. An investigation into the shooting revealed the true purpose of the warehouse, and Logan and Fred Billingsley were promptly arrested. Soon after, Margett was arrested on charges of grand larceny and "accepting the earnings of unfortunate women," thus allowing for a brief lull in the local vice trade.[126]

By June 1917, the federal government had introduced a war tax bill that suspended production by distilleries throughout the United States and established that any bonded whiskey still aging in barrels would be subject to a new tax. Medicinal whiskey and industrial alcohol production were not subject to this law. Also, the Spanish flu pandemic (1918–19) played a pivotal role in the campaign for medicinal whiskey, as physicians used whiskey to treat this epidemic.[127]

Then, on November 5, 1918, Washington voters passed Referendum 10 in favor of the bone-dry legislative act. The vote was 96,100 for and 54,322 against.[128]

The alcohol black market expanded quickly, paving the way for the first wave of regional bootleggers, with regular arrests throughout the state by local police and federal agents (also known as G-Men, the underground slang used during Prohibition for any government agent).[129] As a bizarre arrest at the county stockade at the Willows proved, one could even find illicit stills operating inside a prison.[130]

As we head into the Prohibition era, you might as well keep on drinking. After all, throughout most of Washington State, folks were boozing it up. So why not join the club (that is, assuming you know the proper password)?

Chapter 3

PROHIBITION IN "WET" WASHINGTON STATE

The Eighteenth Amendment to the United States Constitution prohibited the manufacture, sale and transportation of alcoholic beverages and their import into or export from the United States and all its territories. The United States Congress passed this amendment on December 18, 1917, but for this amendment to become operative, it required the ratification of three-fourths of the states. Washington State was the twenty-second state to ratify the Eighteenth Amendment, on January 13, 1919, by a unanimous vote in both the state house and senate. Three days later, the United States Congress ratified the Eighteenth Amendment, and it went into effect on January 17, 1920.

On October 28, 1919, Congress adopted the National Prohibition Act, designed to enforce the Eighteenth amendment. This act, which became known as the Volstead Act after Representative Andrew J. Volstead (R-MN), declared all liquors with more than half of 1 percent alcohol to be intoxicating and banned the manufacture, sale, barter, transport, import, export and possession of alcohol.[131] Less than a week after the passage of the Volstead Act, the term *Volsteadian* came into use to describe Prohibition-era laws about alcohol.[132]

Legal Consumption of Alcohol During Prohibition

Select exemptions under the Volstead Act permitted one to imbibe legally. For example, one could still obtain liquor with a medical prescription, though in the first five years of Prohibition, only twenty-six states (including Washington State) allowed the sale of medicinal liquor. Pre-Prohibition, the American Medical Association (AMA) started questioning the efficacy of medicinal liquor and whiskey in particular. But once Prohibition went into effect, in a 1921 AMA survey,[133] 51 percent of U.S. physicians were now in favor of prescribing whiskey, with fifteen thousand doctors lining up for permits within the first six months of Prohibition.

In *Last Call: The Rise and Fall of Prohibition*, Daniel Okrent summarized the process for obtaining such "medicine":

> *For most of the 1920s, a patient could fill a prescription for one pint every ten days, and a doctor could write one hundred prescriptions a month on numbered government-issued forms that resembled stock certificates and were as dearly cherished. Although there were many regional differences, the tab was generally three dollars to purchase the prescription from a physician and another three to four dollars to have it filled. Dentists were similarly licensed, as were veterinarians, who believed their patients could use a belt of Four Roses.*[134]

These guidelines were considered so restrictive that many legitimate druggists chose to close shop rather than pursue a permit. "We used to sell liquor upon a physician's prescription. Prescriptions were filled in the same manner as those for drugs. There were no precautions to be taken, no stringent rules to observe and no laws that might be evaded. The text of the Enforcement Act makes it impossible, however, for us to continue the sale of liquors," a source told the *New York Times*.[135]

Under the Volstead Act, any liquor purchased before January 17, 1920, could be consumed at home. Private social clubs and individuals of means and available space amassed collections of fine wines and liquors that would rival any well-stocked bar, with liquor stores across the United States announcing "going out of business" sales.

In keeping with the spirit of allowing mild consumption of alcohol in private, the Volstead Act permitted home winemaking and brewing. Soon after national Prohibition began in the 1920s, a person could walk into

Prescription for medicinal liquor issued under the authority of the National Prohibition Act. *Courtesy of Mike Gifford/Blackfish Spirits Distilling.*

virtually any grocery store in the United States and find for sale brick-sized blocks called Vine-Glo: compressed raisins bound together with condensed grape juice. Attached to the block was a small container of dried yeast. The wrapping contained the following text:

> *WARNING: Do not dissolve this fruit brick in warm water and then add the contents of the yeast packet, as this will result in fermentation and the creation of alcohol, the production of which is illegal.*[136]

Along those lines, the Volstead Act banned the sale of beer but not the ingredients for making suds. Although malt syrup was advertised as a baking ingredient, many buyers used the extract to make beer. An in-store cardboard sign display for a Budweiser-brand barley malt syrup even featured a grocer winking knowingly at customers.[137]

Also, liquor could be used for sacramental and religious purposes, though no statistics exist regarding how many Washingtonians suddenly "got religion" during Prohibition.

THE CANADIAN CONNECTION

Under Canadian law, local distillers could make spirits for sale to the United States so long as those purchasing their spirits paid an export tax of twenty dollars per gallon. Several large distilleries opened in Vancouver, British Columbia, to serve the West Coast.[138] In late 1920, the Canadian government suddenly realized how much alcohol revenue was being earned by these various export houses, courtesy of the American bootleggers, and decided to raise the annual licensing fees for these liquor-exporting businesses from $3,000 to $10,000.

In response, the top Canadian export houses pooled their resources and formed Consolidated Exporters Limited, which became the single largest supplier of Canadian booze for the entire Pacific Northwest region. It opened offices in Seattle, Portland and San Francisco, establishing a formal network of contact men (otherwise known as land agents) up and down the West Coast. To remain as discreet as possible, Consolidated Exporters went to great lengths to legally disguise itself as well as its American customers. At its first meeting, the acting directors all agreed to burn the company books at the end of each year to protect the nature of its business. A special filing system was used where the names and addresses of top customers were either coded or kept intentionally vague, and the land agents were instructed to never hold a meeting in the same place twice.[139]

As expected, the U.S. government pressured Canada to stem the flow of liquor coming from Canada to the United States. Finally, the Canadian government passed a law in 1930 banning foreign customers from purchasing booze directly from export houses. In response, Consolidated Exporters purchased three gigantic fishing boats to surreptitiously carry huge loads of booze out to the Haro Strait, just outside U.S. territorial waters, where rumrunners could secretly rendezvous with them. These Canadian "motherships," as they became known, acted as floating warehouses of booze anchored out on the open waters. Most American smugglers preferred this, as it eliminated any official record of them buying anything illegal.[140]

THE EVERGREEN STATE'S RUMRUNNERS AND BOOTLEGGERS

While both rumrunners and bootleggers were engaged in the transportation of illegal liquor, rumrunners transported their wares via sea, often using high-speed boats designed to evade capture. Bootleggers, who got their name from the practice developed in the 1880s of concealing flasks of illicit liquor in one's boot tops when going to trade with Native Americans, delivered their goods via land.[141]

In the waters of Puget Sound, an active fleet of rum-running ships smuggled liquor from Canada through the Strait of Juan de Fuca and to ports throughout western Washington. The most famous of these Puget Sound rumrunners was Johnny Schnarr, a World War I army veteran who grew up in Chehalis. He made more than one thousand deliveries and held the distinction of being one of the only rumrunners who was never caught, even after having a $25,000 reward offered for his capture.

Schnarr's reputation placed his services in high demand, and he hauled liquor for many of the region's top bootleggers.[142] As an example of his notoriety, when Canada banned sales of liquor to foreigners, Schnarr needed a new ship capable of these new ocean voyages. He was such a valued customer of Consolidated Exporters that they loaned him the money for this new boat, which Schnarr named *Revuocnav* ("Vancouver" spelled backward).[143] This boat was 56 feet long and boasted two 860-horsepower Packard Liberty airplane engines with top speeds of up to 40 knots while fully loaded with 250 cases of booze. Despite these high speeds, as the exhaust pipes were mulled and ran under the boat, the vessel was very quiet.

Once the liquor reached U.S. shores, the contraband would be distributed by area bootleggers. In Tacoma, the top booze trafficker was Pete Marinoff, though everyone knew him as "Legitimate Pete" due to his avoidance of other criminal enterprises such as prostitution, narcotics and gambling. Considered one of the region's shrewdest bootleggers, Marinoff maintained a fleet of seven speedboats that he used to smuggle Canadian liquor into the Tacoma market. In the early days, Marinoff would often pilot his own ships; he later formed a partnership with Schnarr, who served as his top smuggler.[144]

Another former police officer, C.P. Richards, had a "mansion" constructed around 1929 in an area now part of Mukilteo that became known as Smuggler's Cove. Some folklore suggests that the construction of this operation was financed by Al Capone's interests, although no evidence can be found that the famous Chicago gangster ever came to Smuggler's Cove.

This "mansion" was actually the shell of a manor house designed to conceal bootlegging activities. A second nine-by-nine-foot basement built under the first basement had a still and a tunnel connecting the operation to the gulch and Puget Sound in case the smugglers needed to make a quick getaway.[145]

In Seattle, Roy Olmstead (1886–1966), "King of the Puget Sound Bootleggers," dominated the market. Olmstead learned the fine points of liquor smuggling during his years wearing the badge as a police lieutenant pursuing and arresting rumrunners.[146] After his dismissal from the force for smuggling liquor, Olmstead, along with his wife, Elise; engineer Al Hubbard; and lawyer Jerry Finch set up shop in Smith Tower, then the most modernized building in the city, where he hobnobbed with Seattle's well-heeled business class.[147]

Olmstead scrupulously guarded the integrity of his products as he catered to Seattle's upper class. During the height of Prohibition, his extensive, well-organized operation delivered two hundred cases of Canadian liquor to Seattle every day and grossed $200,000 a month. Further establishing himself as a savvy and brilliant businessman, Olmstead avoided paying Canadian export duty tax on his liquor by taking advantage of a trade agreement between Canada and Mexico. By falsifying and forging documents, he made it look as though his liquor was heading for Mexico, thus avoiding the $20-per-case duty tax. This enabled him to undercut his competitors by as much as 30 percent and establish his dominance in the local market.

Brad Holden, author of *Seattle Prohibition: Bootleggers, Rumrunners & Graft in the Queen City*, observes how Pacific Northwest bootleggers were markedly different from their Eastern counterparts.

> *There were no gun battles over turf or massacres like those seen in New York, Chicago and St. Louis. Bootleggers in the Puget Sound region tended to approach the trade as entrepreneurs rather than mobsters. This level of civility was on display in March 1922, when a bootleggers convention was held at a Seattle hotel. Utilizing Robert's Rules of Order, more than 100 bootleggers formally established rules and protocols for their profession and then celebrated together afterward.*

During this same year, Edwin "Doc" Brown was openly campaigning for mayor of Seattle. The sixty-year-old ex-dentist, known for his youthful energy that was accentuated by a head full of thick, dark hair, was very vocal about his opposition to the Eighteenth Amendment. Surprisingly, Brown did not personally imbibe.

Immediately on assuming office, Brown let it be known that if the federal government wanted Prohibition enforced, then federal agents should enforce it themselves. He also believed that imported alcohol was safer than

A display depicting Roy Olmstead's offices at Smith Tower. *Photo credit: Becky Garrison.*

street-level moonshine and ordered his police force to concentrate on people selling "bad booze" rather than harass any of the bootleggers conducting business in Seattle.[148]

Just as those running moonshine in the South jacked up their cars so they could evade law enforcement (thus launching the birth of NASCAR), engineer Al Hubbard built the fastest speedboats aided by Boeing technology.[149] Nearby Boeing Airfield was full of surplus aircraft left over from World War I, and parts could be purchased for cheap. So far, there is no direct evidence that William Boeing participated in Olmstead's smuggling operations other than serving as one of Olmstead's clients.[150] Along those lines, Boeing lived in the Highlands, an elite gated community in Seattle overlooking the bluffs. According to oral accounts, the foot of these bluffs became a well-known drop point for rumrunners, but Boeing's connection, if any, to this particular smuggling operation has not been proven.

Also, Hubbard utilized his technical prowess to build KFQX, the first commercial radio station in Seattle, which broadcasted from Olmstead's new palatial home in the Mount Baker section of Seattle. In addition to nightly news and weather broadcasts, Elise aired her popular program *Aunt*

Voran, in which her character would read bedtime stories to a dedicated fan base of local children. This led to the popular urban legend that Elsie was secretly inserting coded messages into these stories to assist her husband's bootlegging operation. This story has been neither proven nor debunked.[151]

The illicit liquor business in Seattle continued unabated until 1924, when Bertha Knight Landes assumed the role of mayor temporarily as Mayor Erwin "Doc" Brown was out of town attending the Democratic National Convention. Federal agents took this as a sign to clean up the town. Olmstead was tipped off, but as he was connected to the most powerful people in Seattle, he ignored the threats. When Mayor Brown returned to Seattle, he reappointed his original police chief, and things were soon restored to normal working order.

Even though agents wiretapped Olmstead's office and home, at that time wiretapping was illegal and could not be used in a court of law. Despite this fact, Olmstead was convicted, and his case went to the Supreme Court, which ruled in a landmark decision that wiretapping was now legal. Olmstead was released from jail on May 12, 1931, and began life anew as a recent convert to Christianity. By the time Olmstead received a presidential pardon, he had already served out his sentence.[152]

PROHIBITION AND THE PILOTS

The 1920s also marked the beginning of the Golden Age of Flight with the introduction of crop dusting in 1924 and Charles Lindberg's famous transcontinental flight from New York to Paris in his Ryan monoplane on May 20–21, 1927.[153] The city of Everett and Snohomish County added an airplane to their law enforcement activities on July 13, 1927, when Chief of Police C.A. Bailey made J.R. Scott chief of the air patrol. Scott's Ryan monoplane was the same type of plane Lindberg used for his transatlantic flight. He flew this plane from its home field in Everett, which was located northeast of the town on a narrow sliver of land on Ebey Island.[154] According to Ernest Troth of James Bay Distillers Ltd. of Everett, rumor has it that in addition to his law enforcement duties overseeing the pilots under his command, Scott made regular flights smuggling spirits from British Columbia. Once he flew into Everett, he would halt midfield and load the booze into cars that drove down State Route 99 (also known as the Pacific Highway) to Seattle.

Ryan monoplane
owned by J.R. Scott.
Courtesy of Ernest Troth,
James Bay Distillers.

While no FAA records of this plane or any Washington State records of Scott's company, "Commercial Air Transport," exist, Troth's research revealed multiple newspaper accounts in the *Bellingham Herald* listing J.R. Scott as the president of Commercial Air Transport,[155] with an article in the *Daily Olympian* reporting that this company was planning a modern commercial airport north of Bellingham that included an air taxi between Everett and Bellingham.[156] A newspaper account in the *Chilliwack Progress* points to the sale of a plane in 1932 to Coote that matches the description of Scott's plane, though Scott is not referenced in this article.[157] According to Troth, the plane burned after it was sold and moved from Bellingham to British Columbia.[158]

An investigation by the *Spokane Daily Chronicle* pointed to the ease with which a Spokane-based aerial bootlegger smuggled booze from across the Canadian border. The pilot only had to stow some extra gasoline in the cargo compartment, fly over the border, load up eighteen cases of whiskey and pour the extra gas in the tank for the flight back. This entire operation took less than three and a half hours. If the pilot saw officers waiting at the designated landing spot, he could simply land someplace else. If officers showed up later, while the plane was being unloaded, the pilot could restart the engine, wave goodbye to the onrushing Prohibition agents and take to the sky. Should the pilot run into engine trouble, he just needed to trade some whiskey to some bystanders for new spark plugs or help with repairs and was soon on his way.[159]

Other pilots who smuggled spirits from Canada include Glenn Holt, who was arrested in 1925 when his liquor-laden seaplane was seized at Champagne Bay on Lake Washington. This was followed by a raid on the home of the plane's owner, Lyle H. Swigler, on Victory Highway, resulting in Swigler's detention by federal narcotics and prohibition agents as a rum and narcotics runner. Also, federal authorities found 169 cases of alleged beer at the old Everett Bottling Works (3205 Broadway). They alleged that this beer was manufactured in Everett, though this liquor was not disposed of there but shipped to Seattle, where apparently it was labeled, sacked and marketed as Canadian goods. In addition, when the raiding squad inspected the bottling works' new building at 3231 Broadway, they found several hundred cases of bottled goods, which might have been beer.[160]

In addition, a letter dated May 1, 1928, was sent to Special Agent B.F. Hargrove Jr. with the U.S. Prohibition Service in Seattle calling for an investigation of the smuggling activities of Sterling Traders Ltd. of Vancouver, British Columbia, and its agents. As per information received through a confidential source, these named agents had recently become associated with the Olympic Aeronautic Corporation in Tacoma. Initial inquiries revealed that this newly formed corporation was created for the sole purpose of smuggling liquor into the United States, adding that it recently purchased two new planes from the Eagle Rock Plane Company, in Denver. Apparently, considerable liquor had arrived the past month from Victoria and Vancouver, British Columbia, with these liquor shipments being received by these airplanes at some point in Puget Sound and smuggled into Tacoma.[161]

DISTILLING PROHIBITION-STYLE SPIRITS

Since law enforcement could spot the trails of smoke coming from fires used to heat illegal stills, moonshiners often fermented sugarcane or malt syrup. Unlike raw grains that needed to be cooked prior to fermentation, sugarcane and malt syrup could be fermented at room temperature, thus cutting back on the need for as much firepower. The equipment for illicit distilling was similar to the apparatuses utilized by commercial distilleries, though it's likely the cooling condenser was made from a repurposed car radiator and the still was cobbled together from metals, some of which were very likely poisonous.

Traditionally, distillers make "cuts" (discarding the beginning and end of the run) of the liquid out of the still to ensure they remove the natural acetaldehyde, methanol and fusel oils that form during fermentation. During Prohibition, distillers often skipped that step to save money since they were already committing an illegal act and not putting their names on the bottles anyway.[162]

A rule of thumb for the more unscrupulous distillers was that one bottle of good whiskey could be cut into five bottles of bad whiskey. Most often, the cutting was done in the middle of the night in plants set up in warehouses or storage facilities that looked deserted, and therefore not suspicious, by day. The tools of the cutter's trade were water, flavorings and alcohol. The water increased the quantity of the beverage, the flavorings restored the diluted mixture to something approximating its original taste and the alcohol replaced the lost pizzazz.

As expected, the alcohol utilized for cutting was subpar at best. Some even turned to industrial (denatured) alcohol since that product was not banned by the Eighteenth Amendment on the grounds it was needed to make chemicals, solvents, insecticides, explosives, fuels and certain cleaning products. Cutters containing denatured alcohol included perfume, cologne, aftershave lotion, mouthwash, hair tonic and shellac—virtually anything made from alcohol, however small the quantity of alcohol contained in that particular product.

Eventually, things got so bad that the government stepped in, with the ASL rooting it on, and ordered manufacturers of many alcohol products to add an emetic to them. Even this new addition of a substance designed to induce vomiting failed to deter moonshiners from using denatured alcohol as a cutting agent. As Burns reflects, "On top of possible blindness or even death, drinkers now had to deal with nausea, courtesy of the federal government."

Burns notes how antifreeze was a favorite cutting agent. Moonshiners "claimed it was a flavorful additive, especially when it had been newly drained from an automobile radiator because the pieces of rust in it gave the solution a rich, full body. Not to mention, one assumes, needed iron."

According to Burns, poisoned booze was the great unsung tragedy of Prohibition.

People today know about bootleggers and speakeasies; they are familiar with the names Capone and Kennedy, and they have a general impression of casual lawbreaking and wild times kindled by spirits that were not supposed to be so readily available. But they do not know about Yack Yack Bourbon, Jackass Brandy and Squirrel Whiskey. They do not know about cooking alcohol squeezed through a rag and mothballs dropped into a steaming mug of gasoline. And they do not know about Jamaica gin and the men who drank it in doses that were so much more than minute, thereby getting rid of their thirsts for a few minutes as they turned into cripples for the rest of their lives.

Even men and women who could afford better were sometimes the victims of deadly drink; it could find its way into the best of night spots, the most soigné of private parties, the most respectably labeled and highly-priced bottles, the finest crystal. Anyone, at any time, could be fooled by a bootlegger.[163]

In the saloon era, calling for liquor by brand name was almost unheard of; in the speakeasy era, it became a habit, first as a means of protecting oneself from alcohol of questionable origin and secondarily as a way of expressing one's level of taste. Decades later, many of the liquor industry's best-known brand names owed their prominence to the ubiquity of Prohibition-era rotgut. But as Okrent observed, knowing one's brand did not ensure one was drinking said brand. "In too many places, if you ordered Brand X, you got Brand X; if you ordered Dewar's or Gordon's, you paid twice as much and got Brand X."[164]

The first published definition of a cocktail appeared in an editorial response in the *Balance and Columbian Repository* of 1806. It read: "Cocktail is a stimulating liquor composed of spirits of any kind, sugar, water and bitters."[165] During Prohibition, cocktails were designed to obscure the vile taste of spirits like bathtub gin, a homemade and often poorly made spirit. Often, this gin was made in a bottle so tall that it could not be mixed with water from a sink tap and had to be mixed in a bathtub instead. Though its name references gin specifically, *bathtub gin* came to be used as a general term for any type of cheap homemade booze. Also, there was white lightning, which was the whiskey equivalent of bathtub gin. (These whiskeys were typically unaged, as hanging on to illicit spirits while they aged risked detection by local law enforcement.) All were highly potent, illegally made and poor-quality spirits.[166]

WASHINGTON STATE'S INFAMOUS MOONSHINERS

Among those Washington State moonshiners operating during this era, Seattle restauranteur Frank Gatt stands out as one of the best and most brazen. Mayor Brown was considered a close friend of his, and there was even an unsubstantiated rumor that Gatt ran a still in the basement of Brown's home.

Gatt came up with the brilliant idea of operating his stills out of rural dairy farms where the strong cattle smell would offset any odors created by

Left: John Bates (*left*) (1867–1958) was the manager of the Washington Hotel in Ellensburg from 1923 to 1938. Rodney Rankin (*right*) was living in Kittitas County by 1910. He was known as "Alkali Ike" and operated an automobile service station near Vantage by the Columbia River and was a well-known bootlegger during Prohibition. His stills were located on the left side of the Vantage Highway on Saddle Mountain. He was arrested several times and spent time in prison. Rodney died on May 8, 1954, in Lee County, Iowa. *Courtesy of Ellensburg Public Library.*

Below: The Borrows Hotel (Pearl Street and Second Avenue, Ellensburg) was built soon after the July 4, 1889 fire. Owned and operated by members of the Frederick Borrow family until the mid-1950s, the lodging house served the community for many years. In the 1920s, the Old Brick, as it was called, was a much-sought-out speakeasy. The city mayor or local sheriff would let Kate Borrow Hinman know when there was to be a liquor raid. When an officer of the law stopped by the hotel, all the guests were drinking coffee or tea. *Courtesy of Ellensburg Public Library.*

the moonshining process. Also, the farms tended to be remote enough that they were far off the beaten path of any nosy deputies. Gatt's first purchase was the Nelson Dairy Farm. The Nelson family continued to live and work at the small, humble farm, operating their dairy business as usual, which gave the illusion that nothing illegal was taking place there.

Meanwhile, Gatt's moonshine crews began operating two massive stills on the property, the largest of their kind in the entire Pacific Northwest. Each still had a capacity of five hundred gallons, with enormous vats to store the liquor after it was made. The booze would then be bottled, loaded into one of Gatt's cars and driven under the darkness of night to his various restaurants in downtown Seattle. After two attempts to convict him, Gatt was sent to prison; on his release, he set up large-scale stills in Renton, Tacoma and Lake Washington. There were even reports of Gatt opening up an illegal nightclub in Port Townsend, complete with booze, gambling and live jazz bands.

One night, as Gatt was leading a small caravan of vehicles on a delivery run, he was pursued by what appeared to be federal agents. A high-speed chase ensued, with both sides exchanging gunfire. The crew got away, though his brother Jonny was wounded and became wheelchair-bound, and the guilt from this incident haunted Gant until his dying day.[167]

While no one else reached Gatt's scale of operation, local newspapers were chock-full of stories detailing raids against myriad "scofflaws" who engaged in the illicit liquor trade. (This term arose out of a 1924 contest to devise a word that defines those who violated Prohibition liquor laws.)[168] The black market in Aberdeen was controlled by moonshine kingpin Chris Curtis,[169] while over in Spokane, federal officials called Albert Commellini the "king of moonshiners."[170]

Those arrested for possession of liquor with the intention to sell tended to get off with a fine and their goods confiscated (unless, of course, these bootleggers or rumrunners chose to resist arrest and the situation became violent). Similar scenarios transpired with those arrested during the many raids on speakeasies and other places serving illegal spirits. (Side note: While the term *speakeasy* is used today to refer to a place that sold liquor illegally during the period of Prohibition in the United States, the earliest citation for a speakeasy came from Australia, almost one hundred years earlier.)[171]

Often, these stories were accompanied by photographs of dry men smashing stills or standing before their haul of confiscated stills with the swagger of a big game hunter who just bagged his prized kill. Having said

This photo was taken in 1930 of the popular Lattice Inn located on the bank of the Yakima River, fifteen miles south of Ellensburg and twenty-two miles north of Yakima. It was owned and operated by W.J. Burns. Old-timers remember the Lattice Inn being a wild place during Prohibition. *Courtesy of Ellensburg Public Library.*

that, even a small fifteen-gallon still could be confiscated if the Dry Squad was so inclined.[172]

When necessary, dynamite would be employed, such as in the case of an illicit operation at Five-Mile Prairie, a neighborhood on the far north side of Spokane. This facility was described as the largest booze and alcohol factory in this part of the state. Two days of work with giant powder were required to jolt the stills into ruins, and the operation sounded like a Fourth of July celebration. As reported by the *Spokesman-Review*, "fortunately, permission was granted for the removal of hogs and chickens from the scene, or the mortality would have been great."[173]

Even a place like Vashon Island, which was a stronghold of temperance activity pre-Prohibition, found itself awash in illegal liquor. In *A Brief History of Vashon Island*, author Bruce Halman notes how Vashon College bragged in its promotional brochures, "There are no saloons, gambling houses, dance halls or other places of evil influence within eight miles of Vashon College." Along those lines, many islanders joined the Vashon Island Eighteenth Amendment Society to fight the repeal of Prohibition and sponsored a well-attended "Dry Parade" in October 1932.

Confiscated copper stills at the courthouse in Port Angeles, 1923. *Courtesy of the Kellogg Collection of the North Olympic Library System.*

This photo, dated May 20, 1921, is from the files of McFaden Photo Co. and was taken near the sheriff's office and county jail in Walla Walla. *Courtesy of Bygone Walla Walla (wallawalladrazanphotos.blogspot.com).*

That said, during Prohibition, there were numerous raids on stills, and nighttime movements of boats running alcohol were a regular sight. Vashon voted to become wet in August 1933, 403 to 313, and the Beach Tavern, at the foot of the Heights Dock, opened as the island's first legal bar.[174]

Not only did Prohibition mark the first time women drank in public, but during that era, they were also arrested for participating in the illicit liquor biz. Take the case of Black Mary, the reputed queen of the foothill bootleggers. While the date of the Black Diamond rum raid is unknown, according to a reliable anecdotal account, Division Prohibition Chief F.A. Hazeltine and a squad of federal agents seized approximately two thousand gallons of contraband beverages and arrested Mary Draghi, described as a comely twenty-five-year-old maiden, along with her father, Pete Draghi; Aniceti Magnan; Nello Merlino; and brothers Carlo and Leo Fontana.

In raiding four establishments, the basements of which were fitted up after the manner of public drinking rooms in France, the feds seized and then smashed 1,500 bottles of beer, 400 gallons of homebrew, 800 gallons of wine and a quantity of moonshine. They wrecked the works, and those four basements were veritable pools of beer and wine when they finished. The work of smashing the first establishment took so long that the operators of the three other houses were frantically destroying their liquor when the squad arrived to relieve them of the job. No patrons of the four "taverns" were arrested.[175]

Also, the largest moonshine still captured in Seattle in 1924 belonged to another young woman, Mrs. Theresa Jones, twenty-eight. When the Dry Squad raided her house at 9948 Fifty-First Avenue, they found the house was completely equipped as a first-class distillery. Mrs. Jones was dressed as though going to a party when the police entered. She took off her hat when she saw the policemen and told them where to find the still and the liquor. After her arrest, she was released on $500 bail.[176]

Lost in the public tales that hit the presses were the quieter stories of folks trying to eke out a living in the mines, at the sawmills or on the farms. Prohibition allowed them to enhance their meager incomes by working as rumrunners, bootleggers and moonshiners. For example, a resident who grew up in Ronald recounted how, during Prohibition, the miners made more money in the bootlegging business than in their mining jobs. He said the Slovaks were the whiskey providers, while the Italians were specialists in winemaking.[177]

Then there's the untold story of the Nesset Family Farm, the only remaining intact Norwegian farmstead in Whatcom County once farmed by Norwegian

Nesset relations and friends sip moonshine from a keg set on an old cedar stump behind the Nesset barn. The gentleman to the left is Gus Berg, who was a barber in Bellingham and married one of the Nesset daughters. On the right is Tom Nesset's cousin (and best friend) Gilbert Fidjeland, who worked whaling in Alaska. The other men are unidentified, though most likely they purchased this keg and offered to share a bit of their bounty. This photo was taken by Tom Nesset, co-owner of the Nesset Family Farm. *Courtesy of the Nesset Trust.*

immigrant homesteaders. For decades, they worked tirelessly to coax a living from the land, raise five children and run a small dairy. In the meantime, they documented the many pleasures of settler life in the South Fork, including hiking and skiing on Mount Baker and fishing on the Nooksack River.

The Nessets were a devout family, with Tom's grandfather launching a religious revival in Norway. Despite their deep religious convictions, they turned to moonshining during Prohibition, presumably as a means of keeping their farm afloat. Even though Tom kept very detailed recipes and records for everything he did, from fishing for salmon to trapping animals, there's no record of the recipe he used to make his moonshine. Given they grew barley but not corn, one can presume Tom distilled whiskey from barley. Also, Pfeiffer-Hoyt recounted that Tom's sister made dandelion wine and his great-grandfather made blackberry wine.[178]

Other untold stories abound of those distilling off the grid during Prohibition; however, many families I spoke with chose to keep such family matters private, at least for now. Once Prohibition ended, most folks more or less exited the liquor business, though some continued to make homemade wine, beer and cider even though producing these items without a license was now technically illegal.

The Repeal of Prohibition—Kinda, Sorta

In 1926, Seattle elected Bertha Knight Landes as mayor, making her the first big-city woman mayor in the United States. She took drying out Seattle so seriously that speakeasies fled across the city line. One elegant speakeasy that opened in 1929 outside the city limits was the China Castle at Eighty-Seventh and Lake City Way. It had a two-tiered lookout for spotting federal liquor agents and an underground tunnel to a motel across the highway where prostitutes plied their trade. Renamed the Jolly Roger in 1934, the rat-infested building burned in 1989 and is now the site of a gas station. When Landes ran for reelection as mayor in 1928, she was easily defeated by Frank Edwards, a political unknown. Her defeat was a sign of changing sentiment pertaining to the efficacy of Prohibition-era laws.[179]

On November 8, 1932, voters passed State Initiative Measure 61 by a 62 percent margin. This initiative repealed all of Washington's liquor laws except for the prohibition on the sale of alcohol to minors.[180] Local ordinances restricting liquor were quickly repealed, not only in Seattle but also in locations as varied as Yakima and Aberdeen. Beer was available across the street from public schools. Free lunches appeared on the polished mahogany, as did "whisky-flavored tonics" with an alcoholic content in excess of 40 percent. There were taxi dancers, service to minors and shootings. Roadhouses were wide open and attractive to drunks and prostitutes. Moonshine booze under fake labels was a standard item in many drugstores. It was like an old-fashioned whiskey feast that even some cynics found depressing. Federal regulation was limited, except for some coverage under the National Recovery Administration (NRA) codes. The NRA codes regulated prices and business practices separately for each industry, including the beer, wine and distilled spirits industries.[181]

National Prohibition was still in effect until December 5, 1933, when Utah became the thirty-sixth state to vote for the Twenty-First Amendment repealing Prohibition.[182] Washington State ratified this amendment on October 3, 1933.

The debate over alcohol shifted from whether Prohibition should be repealed to how to tax and regulate the sale of alcohol and distilled spirits in particular. These conversations failed to stem the tide of illegal liquor. According to a veteran Prohibition agent, as quoted in the *Spokesman-Review*, "Repeal of the Eighteenth Amendment will decrease bootlegging by two-thirds, but the other third will continue to be a big problem." In his estimation, unlicensed still operators could afford to make a product that compared favorably with bonded whiskey and sell it for $1.50 a quart. He predicted that legal whiskey would cost more than three dollars a quart at retail, adding that some illegal operators were making whiskey as good as or better than the legal article. He cited as one example a Yakima distiller who produced an excellent fruit brandy aged for two years that he could sell for five dollars a quart.

This agent added that another source of cheap, untaxed liquor after Prohibition would be drugstores that mixed five gallons of alcohol, five gallons of water, one gallon of Bourbon and some glycerin to get eleven gallons of whiskey that they could sell at an enormous profit at three dollars a quart or less. Also, in the larger cities, the veteran agent predicted that alcohol stills would be operated secretly to produce gin as good as the legal spirits.[183]

For those wishing to pick up your next cocktail, be mindful of your liquor so that you don't consume some of the more spurious spirits. Also, while Prohibition may have legalized alcohol, liquor has now become highly regulated, with federal, state and local governments dictating your drinking options.

Chapter 4

LEGISLATING LIQUOR

With the passage of the Twenty-First Amendment ending national Prohibition, the issue arose regarding how to best prevent the corrupt, saloon-dominated, freewheeling alcohol era from making a comeback. John D. Rockefeller Jr., a nondrinking Baptist who had earlier been a heavy donor to the antiliquor cause, funded a study group in 1933 to explore how to best address this "alcohol problem." While the group recommended that Prohibition be repealed, they advocated for strict government control of alcohol sales, preferably through state stores where the states could make profits.[184]

In response, the federal government adopted a three-tier system that permitted each state to develop a structure of checks and balances that provided safe alcohol to the consumer while ensuring a simple method to collect tax revenue. The three-tier system is simple in theory: manufacturers provide alcoholic products to wholesalers, who distribute the products to retailers, who sell them to consumers. Under most state models, no entity can be involved in more than one tier, with each tier regulated and licensed separately.[185]

FORMATION OF THE WASHINGTON STATE LIQUOR CONTROL BOARD

In Washington State, Governor Clarence Martin signed the Steele Act on January 23, 1934, which established the Washington State Liquor Control Board (WSLCB, renamed the Washington State Liquor and Cannabis Board, or LCB, in 2015).[186] Governor Martin charged the board with the responsibility of controlling public access to alcohol by restraining competition. This was to be accomplished by regulating the legal manufacture and distribution of alcohol within the state and by licensing the sale of alcoholic beverages in restaurants and hotels, with explicit standards regulating the required ratios of food to beverage sales.[187]

As Clark observes in *The Dry Years*, this act was an effort to solve both the problems of Prohibition and repeal by legitimizing drinking within the context of an antisaloon state. It allowed cities and counties outside the cities a local option to prohibit public drinking, a clause that pleased the rural areas. But the bill gave the state complete power to license the manufacture, wholesaling, retailing and distribution of alcohol, a clause that infuriated many mayors and councilmen from cities that, before Prohibition, had raised as much as half of their revenues from the license fees paid by saloons.[188]

Under the Steele Act, the saloon was gone, as businesses were prohibited from displaying signs or advertising using the words *bar*, *barroom* or *saloon*,[189]

Members of the WSLCB and Governor Martin, 1934. *Courtesy of Washington State Archives.*

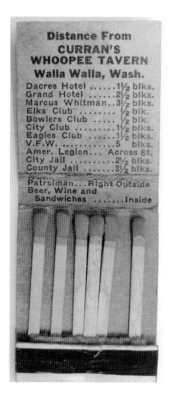

Distance From
**CURRAN'S
WHOOPEE TAVERN**
Walla Walla, Wash.
Dacres Hotel .....1½ blks.
Grand Hotel .....2½ blks.
Marcus Whitman..3½ blks.
Elks Club .... ½ blk.
Bowlers Club .... ½ blk.
City Club ....1½ blks.
Eagles Club .....1½ blks.
V.F.W. ....5 blks.
Amer. Legion... Across St.
City Jail ....2½ blks.
County Jail ......3½ blks.
Patrolman...Right Outside
Beer, Wine and
Sandwiches ......Inside

This matchbook is from Whoopee Tavern (Alder Street, Walla Walla), which was in operation from the 1930s to 1960s. Like a growing number of dining and drinking establishments, it served beer and wine but not hard liquor. *Courtesy of Bygone Walla Walla (wallawalladrazanphotos.blogspot.com).*

as well as running ads showing anyone actually consuming alcohol or depicting women or children.[190] To quote Forsyth, "Repeal legalized the speakeasy; it legalized the restaurant that wanted to serve a glass of wine; it helped out the cruise liner business, but it did not bring back the saloon. Prohibition had worked."[191]

As per their initial regulations, taverns could sell beer (and later wine) by the glass. Hard liquor was not permitted to be consumed in public. The board was empowered to license grocery stores to sell packaged wine and beer, but hard liquor could only be sold through state-owned liquor stores. This purposely created a monopoly on liquor, with profits to be divided between the state's general fund and Washington's thirty-nine counties.[192]

Initially, the board sold hard liquor at a low markup to discourage bootlegging and controlled sales through state-operated "dispensaries." Customers were given a permit number and had to go to a state liquor store to purchase the liquor from a sales agent who stood behind a wired teller box, much like the old postal operations. The customer ordered the liquor by brand and signed a document that the agent kept at the counter.[193]

WASHINGTON STATE'S FIRST LICENSED DISTILLERY POST-PROHIBITION

In January 1934, the first distillery in Washington State after Prohibition began production in Seattle. Northwest Distilleries Inc. (17233 Westland Avenue North) was located in a three-story building, where it boasted $150,000 worth of equipment. This distillery had a rated capacity of two thousand gallons per day and employed, at different times, between twenty and fifty people. The first two products it offered were Mello Smooth Dry

Gin and Mello Morn Straight Bourbon, which both originally sold for sixty-five cents a "fifth" (one-fifth of a gallon). From there, the firm added Briar Springs Straight Blended Whiskey, Princess Pat Sloe Gin and Prince Henry Dry Gin.[194] From its inception, Northwest Distilleries' slogans "Buy Washington" and "Union Made…Washington Made"[195] spoke to its commitment to use materials and services from Washington State whenever possible.[196]

The corporation disappeared from Polk's *Seattle City Directory* after 1939, and the last known mention of Northwest Distilleries is from a 1943 Washington Supreme Court case. Former distillery treasurer Carl Rubinstein sought compensation from a cold storage company that allegedly lost nine barrels of whiskey. The Supreme Court found that the defendants were not liable for the lost product. After that defeat, the distillery disappeared from the scene.[197]

Given that the board has since lost all records of Northwest Distilleries, we cannot ascertain the exact reason for its permanent closure, though one can surmise that launching any business in the midst of the Great Depression would have been tricky at best. At this time, distilling was concentrated in Illinois and other grain-growing areas of the Midwest, which enjoyed economies of scale that could not be replicated in the Northwest. Also, Washington was traditionally viewed as a major brewing state, with 83 percent of the beer consumed in 1936 produced in-state and the state exporting twice as much beer as it imported. As a side note, no one thought of this state as a logical place to make quality wine.[198]

Furthermore, operating any distillery during this era was not for the faint of heart given the amount of regulation required to run a distillery in the United States. After Prohibition, government gaugers locked the stillhouse, cistern room and all the warehouses. The gauger had a key, and the distillery had a different key, making each section double-locked. If workers repaired equipment, the gauger crimped a metal tag after the job. This government oversight kept distillers on their toes but was discontinued in the early 1980s.[199]

WASHINGTON STATE GETS INTO THE BOOZE BUSINESS

In October 1934, the board opened a bottling plant to help satisfy the clamor for quality legal whiskey post-Prohibition. By purchasing good Scotch in bulk and bottling it in Seattle, the board was able to undersell all the good whiskeys on the U.S. market.[200] In addition to their Two Seal and Three Seal brands of Scotch, on occasion, the board bottled gin and wine, as well as rum, brandy and Canadian whisky.

During this time, the board worked with the army and navy to control alcohol sales and consumption on military bases, as well as to deal with the great waves of migrants arriving from 1941 to 1945 to work in wartime industries based in Washington State. The army took over the board's Seattle warehouse, bottling plant and laboratory. In another wartime move, Japanese,

A bottle of blended Scotch whiskey imported and bottled by the WSLCB. *Bottle courtesy of Keith Barnes/Bainbridge Organic Distillers. Photo credit: Becky Garrison.*

Italian, Bulgarian, Hungarian, German and Romanian citizens who held liquor licenses were required to surrender them.[201]

In what might be the most unique distillery sale in American history, the States of Oregon and Washington purchased Kentucky's Shawhan Distillery and Waterfill & Frazier in 1943 in an effort to meet the growing demand for legal liquor. The states purchased the companies' seventy-eight thousand barrels of whiskey for $6.65 million to sell in their state-owned liquor stores. George P. Lilley, then chairman of the Oregon Liquor Commission, said the states then resold the distilleries to their original owners.[202]

This venture closed in 1967 when numerous commercial firms began importing Scotch in bulk and bottling it domestically and were able to undersell the board's brands.[203]

ILLICIT DISTILLING AND ILLEGAL BARS CONTINUE IN WASHINGTON STATE

The illicit trade of liquor began once again when the Federal War Production Board ordered all distilleries to convert to industrial alcohol and produce no beverage alcohol after October 1942. The board then turned to rationing, issuing a ration card for each of the individual purchasing permits required by the Steele Act. This ration card allowed the permit holder to buy one quart of whiskey a week, an allowance that seemed perfectly equitable and easily enforceable, but suddenly the whiskey was disappearing much more rapidly than the rationing plan projected. To their dismay, board planners soon realized that the Steele Act had not prohibited individuals from possessing more than one permit. This embarrassing problem was quickly solved by the Washington State Legislature.

These liquor regulations failed to deter the efforts of local roadhouses, whose mission had always been centered on evading local law enforcement in order to provide their customers with a good time. They were aided in this mission by those city officials—some of them resenting their loss of the power to license, all of them with Depression-struck budgets and inadequate police departments—who would not or could not assign manpower to enforce the laws against liquor.[204]

Many of these establishments were more than prepared for this new era of the board. For instance, when it came to the matter of hard liquor, many roadhouses creatively sidestepped the new law by allowing guests to smuggle in bottles of liquor, at which point they became known as "bottle clubs."

Customers looking to enjoy a fun evening of dancing, dining and drinking would typically arrive with their own bottle of booze (which was expected to be discreetly kept in a bag on the floor under each patron's table), and the house, in turn, offered a setup. Setups were usually included with the cover charge and consisted of a bowl of ice, a pair of glasses and a quart of whatever mixer the person requested, such as ginger ale, sparkling soda water, fruit juices and so on. As for the new rules that forbade people from walking around with their drinks or required women to be dutifully seated (an effort supposedly designed to curb prostitution), many roadhouse operators were too busy running gambling machines to be bothered enforcing such things.[205]

Private nonprofit clubs could serve drinks to members. Under one plan, members used lockers to store personal bottles. More commonly, clubs pooled members' money to buy and store liquor. Members then obtained individual drinks with chits that clubs entered into record books.[206]

The end of World War II saw a major uptick in these new bottle clubs when servicemen returned from the war. In 1946, the U.S. Supreme Court declared these clubs illegal.[207] This same year, the board reported that its Enforcement Division had made 599 raids and 705 arrests and acknowledged that bottle clubs had become a "major problem."[208]

Photo depicting the scene at an illegal speakeasy located at 420-B Second Avenue. During a holdup by James Green, twenty-eight, three men were killed and seven wounded early on August 3, 1941, in one of the Seattle's wildest shootings in years. Green was wounded in a pistol duel with two policemen, both of whom were shot. *Credit line: ACME. Courtesy of Brad Holden, author of* Seattle Prohibition.

On November 2, 1948, Initiative 171 was passed, approving the sale of liquor by the drink, effective March 2, 1949. Establishments wishing to sell liquor by the drink needed Class H licenses, for which nearly one thousand applications were filed in less than six weeks. The board worked with local authorities in considering these applications, which it wanted to award only to "clean, respectable and conservative places of business" and not to "roadhouses" on public highways.[209]

Furthermore, Blue Laws that prohibited the sale of liquor on Sunday remained on the books until 1966. Then a slow dance started for the next decade until all regulations pertaining to Sunday liquor sales were eliminated.[210] Over time, the legislature repealed laws forbidding people to drink while standing and prohibiting women from sitting on barstools. Subsequently, the board allowed the sale of beer at sports arenas and then began to allow liquor advertising on buses, on Sundays and on daytime television.[211]

By 1968, many members of the public had grown concerned that the board was granting liquor licenses to private clubs that discriminated based on race, creed, color or place of national origin. This public uproar intensified in 1971 when it was revealed that liquor companies routinely gave board members thousands of cases of "sample" liquor, for which they could not account. All three current members of the board, one past member and three other men were indicted for grand larceny, fraudulent appropriation, using their positions to secure privileges, bribery and other alleged offenses. The board's reporting of this sampling scandal does not address the long-term fate of these men, though in the years that followed, attempts were made to regulate the board's samples policy.[212]

Over the years, the impact of chronic public inebriation or illegal activities led to communities, the board and the alcohol industry coming together in 1999 to write the Alcohol Impact Area (AIA) rules. Under these rules, the board had the power to designate a geographic area within a city or town as an AIA, with Pioneer Square having the dubious honor of being designated the first AIA. This designation granted local jurisdictions more time to review liquor license applications and renewals for businesses located inside this AIA, as well as allowing them to request that the board restrict grocery and convenience stores from selling certain types of beers and wines linked to local chronic public inebriation problems (such as high alcohol content, low-cost products) or restrict the hours that retailers can sell to-go.[213]

THE BIRTH OF THE CRAFT DISTILLING MOVEMENT

Despite the rise in Washington State of craft breweries and cideries along with boutique wineries, there was no craft distilling scene in this state until 2007, when Don Poffenroth and Kent Fleischmann launched Dry Fly Distilling in Spokane.[214] Poffenroth was winding down a career in the food industry and was searching for a business he could do in Spokane that embodied the spirit of this city from both a raw material and heart standpoint.

As per Dry Fly's website, this brand "began with Poffenroth and a good friend knee-deep in a Pacific Northwest river, just outside the lie on a scenic bend. The two friends discussed how fortunate they were to live, work and play in one of the most amazing places on earth. That conversation hatched an idea to find a way to share their mutual love of hand-crafted spirits and the natural beauty and purity of the Pacific Northwest."[215]

A Seattle design firm, HL2, graphically brought forward this vision in 2006. According to Poffenroth, another key movement toward this dream of producing distilled spirits came through interactions with the fine folks from Christian Carl in Göppingen, Germany, in 2005. They are the oldest continuous still manufacturer in the world, having been in operation for over 180 years.

Currently, Dry Fly is a 100-percent-grain facility producing vodka, gin and a variety of whiskey products along with a line of RTD (ready to drink) cocktails created from these base spirits. Every product decision they make is framed by being 100 percent locally sourced. Poffenroth defines local as "sourcing grain within thirty miles of the distillery, with 99 percent of all other items coming from within Washington State."

As the first legal grain distillery operating in the state since Northwest Distilling Inc. closed its doors in 1939, Dry Fly was instrumental in the passage of 2008's House Bill 2959 "concerning craft distilleries," which led to the current craft distilling boom.[216] Poffenroth describes how this bill came into being. "We had excellent support from Chris Marr, our local state senator. He listened to our ideas and helped us write the legislation. We then, with the help and support of the Washington Grain Growers Lobby and the Washington Beer Commission, spent a week in Olympia to speak with lawmakers directly. In the end, the bill passed the Washington State senate and house with one abstention."[217]

The Craft Distilleries License established as a result of this law had the following requirements and privileges:

- *Annual license fee is $100 (compared to $2,000 for a distillery license).*
- *Produce 20,000 gallons or less of spirits (this amount has now been increased to 150,000 gallons maximum).*[218]
- *At least half of the raw materials used in production must be grown in Washington State.*
- *Sell spirits of its own production for off-premises consumption—limit two liters per day per person.*
- *Samples—maximum of two ounces per person per day free of charge at the distillery.*
- *Spirits used for samples and off-premises sales must be purchased from the Board.*
- *Requires Mandatory Alcohol Server Training (MAST) and a MAST permit for any person who is involved in the service of samples.*[219]

On November 8, 2011, Washington State voters approved Initiative 1183, which privatized liquor sales statewide,[220] thanks in large part to extensive lobbying by Costco, which donated $22.7 million to this initiative.[221] As per this initiative, all state-run liquor stores ceased operations on June 1, 2012, a move that benefited Costco, Safeway, Trader Joe's and other big-box stores that were at least ten thousand square feet but closed down specialty liquor stores that could not meet this size requirement. To date, this law has not been amended to permit smaller stores to sell liquor.[222]

According to Poffenroth, this bill made Washington State's liquor taxes the highest in the United States by a significant amount, as the state raised the liquor tax to make up for any funds lost by the closing of the state-run liquor stores. "Selling products outside the state is usually more profitable than in-state, and that is a crying shame," he reflected.

So the state that once held the distinction of deliberately lowering the price of alcohol in the hopes of discouraging bootlegging now has the highest liquor taxes in the United States.[223]

When Paul Beveridge (yes, that's his real name) of Wilridge Vineyard, Winery and Distillery of Seattle and Yakima began advocating in 1988 to change the liquor laws so that he could operate a winery and a distillery, a member of the board told him, "They'll never be a distillery at a winery permitted in my lifetime. It will have to happen over my dead body." Beveridge and members of Family Wineries of Washington State began calling the board "the Department of No" after it not only denied his request to operate a distillery but also refused to allow him to use refillable bottles or offer restaurant-type service, even though the latter two activities were not mentioned as prohibited by law.

Beveridge was permitted to use refillable wine bottles after convincing the board of the lack of any specific law banning their use. In 2015, the law pertaining to distilled spirits was amended to permit wineries, breweries and cideries to hold a distilling license, with Beveridge's becoming one of the first wineries in the state to also operate a legal commercial distillery. Initially, he had to set up his distillery in a separate space from his winery, though his businesses can now operate under one roof. Until recently, he could not sell his spirits at any tasting rooms where he was also selling his wines.[224]

At one point, distilleries could sell their wares at farmer's markets, though—as was not the case for beer and wine—they could not offer tastings.[225] This option is no longer available, though distillers can offer tastings at special events hosted by 501(c)(3) or 501(c)(6) nonprofits, though they cannot sell spirits or donate money of any kind (booth fees, sponsorships) at these events.[226] The permission to sell spirits at farmer's markets was revoked by the legislature in 2020.

A temporary order granted during COVID-19 that permitted distilleries to sell to-go cocktails has now become a permanent law. Additional activities permitted at a distillery include axe throwing (with approval of a safety operating plan), spirits delivery, internet sales to consumers, sales outside of Washington State (though limited to those states that allow for the sale of spirits from Washington State) and an outside service area (provided the distillery has leasehold rights to the area and provides interior access to the licensed premises and the area is enclosed with forty-two-inch barriers such as ropes and stanchions, railings or fences).[227] To date, those distilleries wishing to serve food need to apply for an on premise restaurant license.[228]

HOME DISTILLING REMAINS ILLEGAL

In 1978, President Jimmy Carter signed H.R. 1337 into law, which legalized the right of any adult to produce a limited amount of wine and beer for personal and family use and not for sale without incurring the wine or beer excise taxes or any penalties for quantities per calendar year.[229] However, since the Twenty-First Amendment predominantly left regulation of alcohol to the individual states, each state's laws differ regarding the specifics of what one can do as a home winemaker or brewer.

While a quick Google search reveals ample options to purchase stills and other distilling equipment for personal use, making hooch at home remains illegal at the federal level, with penalties varying by state.[230] Interestingly, Alaska, Arizona, Maine, Massachusetts, Michigan, Missouri, Ohio and Rhode Island have state laws that would theoretically make moonshining immediately legal if the federal law were to be changed.[231]

In Washington State, unless one is distilling alcohol solely for use as fuel, "any production, sale or transport of any spirituous liquor without government stamp or seal attached thereto, or who shall operate without a license, any still or other device for the production of spirituous liquor, or shall have in his or her possession or under his or her control any mash capable of being distilled into spirituous liquor shall be guilty of a gross misdemeanor and upon conviction thereof shall upon his or her first conviction be fined not less than five hundred dollars and confined in the county jail not less than six months, and upon second and subsequent conviction shall be fined not less than one thousand dollars and confined in the county jail not less than one year."[232]

In other words, don't try this at home. Having said that, a sizable number of pioneering craft distillers learned their craft via good ol'-fashioned moonshining, often with their father or grandfather showing them how to make the family's "secret recipes."

How to Read a Liquor Bottle

According to regulations established by the Alcohol and Tobacco Tax and Trade Bureau (TTB), a liquor bottle must contain the following information on its label.[233]

- *Brand name*
- *Class or type designation (the TTB has specific guidelines for each spirit category)*
- *Alcohol content*
- *Age statement*
- *Color ingredient disclosures (if any)*
- *Commodity statement (the percentage of neutral spirits and the commodity from which the neutral spirits were distilled)*
- *Health warning statement*
- *Name and address*
- *Net contents*

The TTB's class or type designation allows for some latitude among distilleries to use creative marketing terms like *small-batch*, *handcrafted*, *artisanal* and *locally sourced* to describe their products. Washington State native and founder of Portland-based Westward Whiskey Christian Krogstad notes that while the TTB's enforcement of these rules is neither rigorous nor consistent, the general sentiment is that marketers can prevaricate, but they can't outright lie on a label. He cites whiskey author Chuck Cowdry, who calls distillers who mislead consumers on their labels "Potemkin distilleries" after a fake village that was built in Russia to impress an empress. "The bottom line is that if it doesn't say 'distilled by,' then it wasn't. The honest sourcers will have the information right on the label, and will say 'bottled by' or 'produced by' instead, which is a true statement," Krogstad opines.[234]

Most distilleries tend not to discuss NPDs (non-distiller producers), preferring to give the impression they make all their spirits from grain to glass. But while consumers may think the liquor they are purchasing always originates with the distiller, sourcing or contracting neutral grain spirits from an outside source is a relatively common practice among distilleries. This is particularly true when producing neutral grain spirits such as gin or vodka. Here the distiller's skill comes in their ability to source quality neutral grain spirits, as well as to blend botanicals, fruits, spices and other ingredients to create a unique spirit that can be as delectable as one from a distillery that distills its products from inception to bottle. However, when it comes to spirits like whiskeys that originate with a mash bill, a distiller needs to supervise this product from beginning to end for them to claim it as a spirit they created themselves. That said, one can find some very tasty whiskeys produced by those master blenders who know how to source and mix barrels.

Now that you can decipher the nuances behind a liquor label, it's time to hit the road and sample the range of Washington State's craft spirits.

Chapter 5

THE RISE OF PACIFIC NORTHWEST SINGLE MALT WHISKEYS

Ever since the late Steve McCarthy, founder of Clear Creek Distillery in Oregon, ignited a spirited craft revolution when he distilled the first U.S.-based American single malt whiskey in 1993, a select number of Pacific Northwest distillers have focused on producing award-winning American single malts. A growing number of these distillers hail from the craft brew culture, a background that informs their distilling process: for instance, they may brew their wort similarly to how one brews beer, sans the hops. (The starting point for traditional distilleries is called a "wash.")

These whiskeys speak to the terroir of a particular region, as well as the distiller's unique style.[235] The idea is that the flavor of a food or beverage is in some way determined by the place(s) where it is made and the land where its raw materials have been grown. While the term *terroir* tends to be used to describe the different types of soil used for growing grapes, simply put, *terroir* is "the terrain." The factors that can vary based on a spirit's place of origin include climate, weather, season, topography, geography, proximity to specific flora, soil, subsoils, the place and conditions under which these beverages are stored and even the local traditions and regulations that can affect decisions made by the people who are producing the spirit.[236] Hence, each bottling has a distinctive flavor informed by these elements.

In comparison, Scotch is a spirit born of tradition and known for its heterogeneity and consistency, with brands distinguished by their geography (the Highlands, the Lowlands, the Isle of Islay, Campbeltown and the

Speyside). Every bottle is carefully crafted so that each drop of a particular spirit retains the same consistent flavor. A similar vibe besets its cousin, Irish whiskey, as well as most American single malt whiskeys distilled outside of the Pacific Northwest.[237]

Logging and Liquor:
The Birth of Westland Distillery

Matt Hofmann's passion for exploring the simple yet complex flavors in food and drink and his interest in high school chemistry led him to explore how to produce distilled spirits, with a focus on whiskey. His high school friend, Emerson Lamb, shared his enthusiasm, and they set out in 2008 to educate themselves about the distilling industry. Hofmann left the University of Washington and went to Heriot-Watt University in Edinburgh, Scotland, to study brewing and distilling, while Lamb focused on the business side. Lamb's family, who were in the pulp and paper industry, understood the challenges in launching a very long-term, capital-heavy type of business such as distilling whiskey and agreed to finance this venture.

Beginning construction on the barrel room. *Courtesy of Westland Distillery.*

The completed barrel room. *Courtesy of Westland Distillery.*

Installing the wash still. *Courtesy of Westland Distillery.*

Both Hofmann and Lamb chose to focus on American single malt whiskey because they fell in love with both the whiskey and the fact that Washington State produces some of the best barleys in the world. "We wanted to put Washington State on the map," Hofmann reflected.

Westland Distillery launched in 2010 as the second distillery dedicated solely to producing American single malt, behind Stranahan's in Denver, founded in 2004.[238] Westland's distillation process is very close to a typical Scottish double distillation process, though they do their cuts based on their nose (sense of smell), whereas most distillers, including those from Scotland, rely on factors like ABV, time and temperature.

As per the distillery's website, the Westland house style that emerged during those days was a balanced, barley-forward whiskey that honored tradition but also moved it forward in a new way. All Westland's whiskeys are made from 100 percent malted barley, fermented with a unique Belgian saison brewer's yeast and matured in a variety of cask types—leading to new and distinctly American flavor profiles. From that starting point, each expression offers a variation of a house style that departs from the expected conventions of single malt whiskey in its own way.

In recent years, Hofmann explored the unknown possibilities that can be pursued in crafting a single malt whiskey via Westland's Outpost Range. Westland's Garryana is a series that explores aging whiskey in barrels made from a native species of oak called *Quercus garryana* that is indigenous to the Pacific Northwest. Westland's Colere and Solum series explores how barley and peat, respectively, inform the flavor of its whiskeys. Also, Westland sources barrels from local wineries and engages in barrel exchange programs with breweries to provide unique barrel-finished whiskeys.

The Lamb family sold Westland to Rémy Cointreau USA in 2017, with Hofmann staying on as managing director; he resigned in 2023. Despite this shift, Westland maintains its local ethos through its use of Pacific Northwest specialty malts, Garryana oak and other local products, as well as continuing with the distilling practices begun by Hofmann.[239]

Copperworks Distilling Company: From Suds to Single Malt

On hearing Jason Parker's soft Kentucky drawl, one might assume he grew up with bourbon in his blood. While he appreciates all fine spirits, Parker's passion proved to be not bourbon but barley. Armed with Foxfire books that focused on distilling Appalachian style, he began exploring the art of making booze while still in his teens. He partnered with his high school buddies to create a brewery named Cripple Creek Brewing with the intention of making beer for all their friends who were too young to drink. That venture failed, though he continued perfecting his home-brewing skills with his dad.

These homegrown efforts paid off in 1989, when his beers convinced Charles Finkel to bring him on as Pike Brewing Company's first head brewer.[240] During this time, he connected with his neighbor Micah Nutt over their shared love of home brewing and distilling.

After stints at Fish Brewing Company, Redhook Brewery and Pyramid Brewery, along with degrees in chemistry and microbiology from the Evergreen State College, Parker noticed that while the burgeoning craft beer and boutique winery movements focused on flavor, this criterion had not yet caught on with distillers. Their energies tended to be centered on getting the maximum amount of alcohol out of a pound of grain products. While some opening small craft distilleries in this state were looking to create spirits made with Washington State products, Parker noticed they didn't know how to do a fermentation or build an alcohol beverage plant.

Given his brewing background, he felt he was qualified to jump in and open a medium-sized distillery with a focus on making spirits that were predicated on making great beer. Nutt shared his interest and offered to be his first investor, as well as working at the distillery for the first five years.

When Parker and Nutt opened Copperworks Distilling Company in 2013, they had the distinction of being the first distillery in Washington State to brew what is essentially beer wort in a major capacity. The end result is a spirit that Parker describes as having a "beer-informed palate with malt expressions of a single farm, single variety malts."

Copperworks began distilling whiskey from day one and also produced gin and vodka to pay the bills and entice future customers until its first whiskey (Release 001) was ready for release in 2016. This whiskey was first brewed from two varieties of pale malt before being twice distilled in traditional copper pot stills brought over from Scotland. Initially, Parker and Nutt brewed their wort with Pike Brewing Company, followed by Elysian Brewing Company and Fremont Brewing Company. Recently, they formed a relationship with Talking Cedar Brewery and Distillery to brew their wort there.

Copperworks' innovative practices, such as starting with a beer wort, coupled with its focus on education and environmental commitments with ventures like Salmon-Safe[241] and working with small sustainable farms that

Left: Jason Parker, head brewer, Pike Brewing Company, circa 1989. *Courtesy of Pike Brewing Company.*

Below: Jason Parker riding the copper elephant. *Courtesy of Copperworks Distilling Company.*

Micah Nutt (*left*) and Jason Parker (*right*) in front of the backbar in their tasting room. As per the pamphlet *Seattle's Old Saloons*, "The backbar was, of course, the centerpiece. Usually, there was a fringe-frosted mirror, eight or ten feet high by twenty or twenty-five feet in length, in front of which was a wide shelf holding most of the bourbon, rye, gin and Scotch bottled goods in the house. This shelf became a stage where the proprietor could vent his ingenuity in promoting his own business or approaching sporting events." *Courtesy of Copperworks Distilling Company.*

engage in practices like dry farming, led the American Distilling Institute (ADI) to name Copperworks "Distillery of the Year" in 2018.[242]

By 2019, even though Copperworks had more than 260 barrels of whiskey aging in inventory, the demand for its American single malt whiskey exceeded its supply of mature whiskey. Rather than resort to traditional ways of generating capital, such as private investments or venture capital, Parker and Nutt wanted to explore a way to expand their business that would get their friends, family, customers and other supporters involved as brand ambassadors. They decided to raise money via equity crowdfunding, running three campaigns (as of August 2023) and raising over $3.25 million from over 1,500 investors. This capital was used to increase production and open more barrel warehousing, as well as additional tasting rooms/restaurants, with a tasting room opened in Kenmore in 2023. This method both raised cash for expansion projects and also developed brand ambassadors out of customers-turned-investors.

Moving forward, Parker predicts more distilleries will shift to the hyperlocal focus that made craft beer successful. "Craft breweries serve a ten-block radius. They do this with food, programming like bingo or trivia nights, drag shows, live music and local art on display." Not surprisingly, national brand sales tend to go down when local products emerge on the scene that have a focus on craft sensibility and community building.[243]

Setting the Standards for American Single Malt Whiskey

When Hofmann proposed a meetup of other American single malt distillers at the 2016 American Crafts Spirits Association (ACSA) annual convention in snowy Chicago, Copperworks and Westward Whiskey were among the attendees hailing from the Pacific Northwest. From this meeting, the American Single Malt Whiskey Commission (ASMWC) was founded, with the goal of establishing a standard of identity for "American Single Malt Whiskey." For a distiller to use this term to describe its whiskey, the ASMWC recommends that the spirit fit the following criteria:

- *Made from 100% malted barley*
- *Distilled entirely at one distillery*
- *Mashed, distilled and matured in the United States*
- *Matured in oak casks of a capacity not exceeding 700 liters*
- *Distilled to no more than 160 (U.S.) proof, or 80% ABV*
- *Bottled at 80 (U.S.) proof or more, or 40% ABV.*[244]

As American single malt whiskeys continue to win national and global awards, the ASMWC continues to push for the formal establishment of an "American Single Malt Whiskey" category. Clay Risen of the *New York Times* noted how the proposed American definition is looser than Scotland's famously rigid rules. "Like Scotch, American Single Malt would have to be made at one distillery—hence 'single'—using 100 percent malted barley. But while the Scottish version must be distilled on a pot still and aged for at least three years, neither requirement would exist in the United States. Also, tradition (though not law) dictates that Single Malt Scotch be aged in used casks, usually Bourbon barrels, but no such expectation exists for its American counterpart.[245]

PNW grains used in distilling Westland Distillery's specialty single malt whiskies. *Courtesy of Westland Distillery.*

In 2020, the ADI established the American Single Malt Whiskey category for those whiskeys made according to the ASMWC's proposed statement of identity.[246] Whiskey aficionados who are interested in sampling these spirits would be well advised to keep an eye out for news about "American Single Malt" so they can be kept apprised about the latest developments regarding this newfound whiskey category.

Chapter 6

WASHINGTON STATE'S CRAFT SPIRITS COME OF AGE

With the passage of the 2008 Craft Distilleries License Bill, Washington State experienced a distillery boom similar to the rise of the craft beer industry in the 1990s. From 2007 to 2012, the number of distilleries in Washington State grew from one to over twenty.[247] This number expanded to a reported 108 craft distilleries in 2022; the current number was closer to 80 as of August 2023.[248] This drop in the number of craft distilleries can be attributed to myriad reasons, such as loss of distribution channels, family concerns, inability to survive during COVID-19, rent increases and changes to the liquor or zoning laws that rendered their business model untenable. Also, the higher number includes those who applied for a distillery license that remains active for ten years but decided not to pursue this venture.

From rural farms and country villages to suburban shopping malls and urban centers, one can find distilleries producing a wide range of award-winning spirits that speak to the spirit of the Pacific Northwest as well as the individual distiller's style. (In fact, these spirits have won so many awards that I chose not to list them, as the end result would be a much heftier tome.)

So, come join me on a post-Prohibition road trip as we explore the current Washington State distillery scene, starting in Seattle and ending just north of Spokane.

SEATTLE'S URBAN DISTILLERIES

SODO and Downtown Seattle

In recent years, the four square miles that form the industrial heart of Seattle, called SODO (South of Downtown), have become home to a growing urban community of wineries, cannabis dispensaries, breweries and distilleries. Start the tour at **OOLA Distillery**. Since its founding in 2010, this distillery has grown into one of the largest in Washington State.

When asked why he chose this location for his distillery, Kirby Kallas-Lewis described his experience hitchhiking across the country from the Midwest in pursuit of work in the Alaskan fishing industry. "When I hit Seattle, my jaw dropped. The sun was out, tulips were blooming and Puget Sound and the mountains were stunning. I decided that Seattle would be home one day. So that was how the location was chosen. Not

OOLA, the distillery mascot and namesake. *Photo credit: Nicole Kandi.*

exactly a business decision, but I never regretted living here, even though we tax spirits higher here than in all other states."

OOLA's Waitsburg Bourbon is aged in a warehouse located right up the hill from the waters of Puget Sound, and Kallas-Lewis notes how the beautiful salinity informs OOLA's aging barrels. Also, as OOLA does not heat or cool its aging facility, the state's temperature and climate also influence how its bourbon ages. "Without huge temperature swings, we definitely have to age a couple of years longer than the norm, but it gives us a unique flavor that sets OOLA's Waitsburg Bourbon apart," Kallas-Lewis observes.

Proximity to what Kallas-Lewis describes as "some of the absolute best agricultural land and farmers in the world for growing grains for spirits" enabled OOLA to find a farm for its grains that, like the distillery, is committed to organic sustainability practices such as Salmon-Safe. Also, Kallas-Lewis has a large organic garden where he grows many of the botanicals used in OOLA's gins as well as the flower garnishes for its cocktail program. OOLA's community contributions include working with other local businesses and donating to over two hundred local charitable organizations every year. The new OOLA Capitol Hill expansion consists of a bar/restaurant and bottle shop located in the neighborhood where they started OOLA distillery in 2010. OOLA Capitol Hill's concept is PNW casual fine dining with shared plates that are driven by the seasons and paired with cocktails showcasing OOLA spirits.[249]

Traveling north, one finds **Alphabet Vodka**. Alphabet sources all-natural untouched spring water for its premium corn vodka, made using locally sourced, non-GMO corn. Alphabet's six-time glass-still distilling process produces a unique personalized vodka.[250]

Next up, **2BAR Spirits** strives to embody the pioneering tradition established by founder Nathan Kaiser's family when they launched the 2BAR ranch in Texas five generations ago. When they opened their doors in 2012, no one knew what "craft spirits" meant, let alone that one could make an award-winning delectable whiskey outside of Kentucky or Tennessee. With a single-minded focus on making great whiskey, Kaiser, a self-professed "Bourbon guy," produced the first bourbon in Seattle made with 100% local grains. All of 2BAR's corn and wheat comes from a grower near Yakima, while its malted barley is sourced from Greater Western Malting Company. From bottled in bond and straight bourbon whiskey to bourbon finished in

Nathan Kaiser's father and grandfather at 2BAR Ranch. More than a century ago, the Kaiser family settled in South Texas and established the ranch. Nathan continues his family's pioneering spirit with 2BAR Spirits. *Courtesy of 2BAR Spirits.*

wine or amaretto casks, 2BAR is the place to go for bourbon lovers. Recently, Kaiser added legal moonshine (a.k.a. corn liquor) to its lineup, a tribute to his great-grandfather, who used to moonshine on the ranch. As he notes, "It tastes great." Taste it for yourself, and then decide.[251]

To the north of 2BAR is **Westland Distillery**, profiled in the chapter "The Rise of Pacific Northwest Single Malt Whiskeys," followed by **Glass Distillery**. This distillery has been dedicated to crafting an artisan connoisseur-class® collection of vodka spirits made from the finest wine grapes grown in the Pacific Northwest since its founding in 2012.[252]

Step into **Letterpress Distilling** for a taste of Italy. Founder Skip Tognetti grew up with Italian liqueurs embedded in his DNA thanks to his grandparents and extended family in Rome, where his mother, Angela, was born and raised. His grandfather Amorino's ("little love" in Italian) small liquor shop just off the Piazza Cavour allowed him to see how Italians viewed wines and liqueurs as a central part of their everyday lives.

When Tognetti founded Letterpress Distilling in 2012, he envisioned Italian liqueurs as a niche venture he could support by producing whiskey and gin. When he released his first limoncello in 2013 to rave reviews, he decided to shift his vision by focusing on the liqueurs that informed his childhood, including Amaro Amorino, named for his grandfather Amorino Pinti, and Amaro Amorino Riserva, a reserve variation of Amaro Amorino aged in barrels from local distilleries like Copperworks and 2BAR.

Also, he's likely the only distiller in the United States to distill gentian liqueur, a homemade wine-based liqueur made from a flowering shrub found high in the mountains of Europe. This plant's very bitter root has been used for centuries in digestive medicine and forms the bitter notes found in many amari and other bitter liqueurs throughout Europe and beyond. Tognetti named his version Genziana Fernanda after his mother's favorite cousin, Fernanda, who introduced him to this particular liqueur.

Shortly after opening Letterpress, Tognetti was joined in this venture by his college friend of thirty years, Liz Lyman, who left the corporate world to work full time at Letterpress as production manager and CFO. By having his partner focus on the business and marketing side of the distillery, Tognetti can free up his brain to focus on crafting Italian liqueurs.[253]

Take a short break from distillery hopping to check out two of Seattle's most storied liquor landmarks. First up is the **Central Saloon**, the oldest bar in Seattle, opened in 1892 under the name "Watson's Bros. Famous Restaurant." (FYI: Jules Mae Saloon opened in 1888 in Georgetown, but this area was not part of Seattle at this time.) During its lifetime, this

Left: During Prohibition, Central Saloon's dumbwaiter was used to bring drinks from the respectable looking street-level bar down to the patrons in the lower level who were gambling and drinking out of plain sight. *Photo credit: Becky Garrison.*

Below: Liquor bottles are stored in what was once Central Saloon's post office. *Photo credit: Becky Garrison.*

establishment has gone through multiple name changes and iterations, including being a café, post office, employment hall, speakeasy, brothel and the birthplace of grunge. Acts who have performed here include Alice in Chains, Soundgarden and Nirvana.[254]

Then head over to nearby **Smith Tower** and travel back to the roaring twenties. Follow the stories behind celebrated bootlegger Roy Olmstead; his engineer Al Hubbard; his wife and accomplice, Elise Olmstead; and his crooked attorney Jerry Finch. Then head up to the Observatory Bar for a celebratory roaring twenties themed cocktail.[255]

Before leaving downtown Seattle, be sure to stop by **Copperworks**, profiled in the chapter "The Rise of Pacific Northwest Single Malt Whiskeys."

Elise's Old Fashioned (Copperworks new oak cask finished gin, simple syrup, lime and bitters) served at the Observatory Bar/Smith Tower. *Photo credit: Becky Garrison.*

Queen Anne and Fremont

Hidden in the industrial park near Fisherman's Terminal is one of Seattle's biggest gin distilleries. **Big Gin Distillery** describes itself on its website as "Made in Seattle, Washington. Owned by Hood River Distillers. Big Gin is crafted by bartenders, for bartenders, and designed with old-time ginners and true beginners in mind."

The name Big Gin is a play on the nickname "Big Jim," which was given to the father of Big Gin's founder, Ben Capdevielle. A third-generation distiller, Capdevielle distilled gin as a hobby with his father, who learned the craft from Ben's grandfather. As a former bartender, Capdevielle was able to get feedback from chefs and others in the restaurant industry about his gin recipe, with Big Gin emerging as a go-to gin found on the shelves of many Seattle-area barbacks. In 2011, Capdevielle set up shop in Ballard before moving to its current location six years later, with Hood River Distillers acquiring Big Gin in 2016.

Today, Big Jim's legacy continues with head distiller Alex Myers, who has his own history of being homeschooled in the art of distilling. He's added his own expertise to Big Gin's curiously crafted barrel-finished expressions

Big Gin's R+D still, also known as a moonshine still. *Photo credit: Becky Garrison.*

like Bourbon Barreled Big Gin, Peat Barreled Big Gin and other single-barrel releases, along with a vibrant barrel-exchange program with area breweries.[256] Other sustainable ventures include upcycling their juniper through a company called Neptune, which blends the juniper with sea salt and uses this mixture to season their fish jerky.

Walk around the corner and step inside **Fast Penny Spirits**, a woman-owned and operated, award-winning, certified B-Corp distillery.[257] After working in the digital tech field for over twenty years, Jamie Hunt felt a pull to start a business that would give back to the community. Sparked by her passion for amaro coupled with her Italian heritage, where her family made their own wine for generations, she decided to join the small but growing ranks of distillers making their vision of an American amaro she called Amaricano. As Hunt began working on her amaro recipe, she sought out local ingredients when possible, such as saffron, Rainier cherries and hops grown in Washington State and hazelnuts from Oregon. The end result was one of the few amaros made with hops.

Initially, Hunt subleased space from Steve Stone of Sound Spirits, a distillery founded in 2010 and the first distillery in Seattle since Northwest Distillers closed shop in 1939.[258] After Stone lost his distribution due to the pending Initiative 1183 legislation, he decided to sell his distillery, and Hunt purchased the space.[259]

Their launch coincided with the 2020 COVID-19 lockdowns, which prevented them from selling via traditional channels like restaurants and bars. So they shifted to hosting COVID-compliant events at their tasting room with curbside pickup of spirits followed by a cocktail program.

As one of the few female distillers in Washington State, Hunt seeks to diversify this industry through initiatives such as the Women's Cocktail Collective[260] and remains dedicated to supporting and empowering women and women-identified business leaders, local communities and the hospitality industry. This community-focused ethos continues to inform Hunt's commitment to building community, with a focus on groups working with women and LGBT people. She hosts makers' markets and makes this space available to nonprofits regularly. Also, their Pretty Penny program gives back 3 percent of all bottle sales to nonprofits.[261]

Other distilleries located in the Queen Anne area include **Old Log Cabin Distillery**, which now inhabits the space formerly occupied by Batch 206, replete with a tasting room serving cocktails and snacks along with space to hold private events. As per its website, "This distillery was born on the eve of an ownership transition in 2022, with reverence for E.G. Booz's legendary status and full embrace of the brand's rich heritage, primed for the next generation. Old Log Cabin bourbon whiskey brand's roots reach back to 1840, when a 16-year-old E.G. Booz made his first batch of liquid goodness. During prohibition, the brand was made in Canada and became a favorite import of bootleggers, especially Al Capone's infamous smuggling operations. In 2012 Batch 206 acquired the trademark and reintroduced Old Log Cabin to a new generation of fans."[262]

Down the street is **Skybound Spirits**. Skybound produces its spirits using a custom-built five hundred gallon dual pot still and column that is supported with a modern steam-fired boiler, low-volume testing stills and a custom aging vessel, the Punisher. Its spirits are aged in European and American oak barrels.[263]

Traveling north over the Fremont Bridge and along the portion of the Ship Canal called the Fremont Cut, you'll find **Fremont Mischief**, founded by commercial fisherman and craftsman Mike Sherlock and his fishing friends. They started making whiskey in the 1990s based on a recipe from his wife Patti's great-grandfather John Jacob's journals. Jacob immigrated to Oregon from Holland in 1929 and distilled corn, wheat and rye for neighbors, noting that rye was his favorite. When the 2008 craft law passed, the Sherlocks started Fremont Mischief. Their spirited offerings include John Jacob Rye Whiskey, made using Jacob's recipe.

Consumers coming to their distillery can choose from tastings or their restaurant Mischief on Canal that features a menu created entirely of fresh local foods and hand-crafted cocktails made from spirits distilled on-site. Be sure to check out their book *Spirited Cooking from the Pacific Northwest*, a seasonal guide to utilizing local products, foraged ingredients and hand-crafted spirits by Mischief on Canal's Chef John Wahlke in collaboration with Fremont Mischief Distillery.[264]

GREATER SEATTLE (NORTH)

Moving north, **Wildwood Spirits** in Bothell was founded in 2014 with a Ballard tasting room opened in 2023 by business partners Erik Liedholm and John Howie, owners of John Howie Steak Restaurant and Seastar Restaurant & Raw Bar, both in Bellevue. A developer who was Howie's friend reached out to them about the possibility of opening a casual brewpub in Bothell. They had been working on the idea of a distillery, but they could not pursue this dream until a legislative change permitted restaurant owners to be distillery owners.

The distillery runs on the ethos of a chef (Howie) and a sommelier (Liedholm) with a focus on hyper-local and seasonal ingredients. It sources organic non-GMO grain from farmers in Washington. The Braeburn apples and Douglas fir used as two of the seven botanicals for its gin are from Liedholm's backyard in Ballard. Also, Wildwood collaborated with local coffee importer Mercon Coffee Group to produce a special bourbon barrel coffee roast used in their restaurants. During the height of the pandemic, they produced hand sanitizer for the King County Sheriff's Department, the Department of Fisheries & Wildlife and King County Metro. Also, they donated 10 percent of their sales to Big Table Seattle, which is a foundation to help hospitality workers in need.[265]

Scratch Distillery may have opened in 2015 in nearby Edmonds, but the actual story behind this distillery began in 1987, when Bryan Karrick made his date, Kim, a gin and tonic during their student days at Michigan State University. Their love for each other and gin grew, with Bryan opening an optometry practice and Kim brewing beer and working in wineries before deciding she wanted to make gin on her own terms.

The name "Scratch" refers to their commitment to produce all their spirits from scratch using local ingredients when possible, such as Skagit Valley grains and botanicals from the Salish Crossing complex's garden—they even planted their own Rowan berry trees for use in their amaro. Initially, Kim distilled vodka and gin and now produces over twenty spirits.

Kim's obsession with the infinite combinations of botanicals, coupled with her conviction that everyone can like gin if they just get the opportunity to find their favorite combination of flavors and aromas, led to the creation of her GINiology™ workshops. Kim first led one on December 15, 2015, and has since offered over 1,200 GINiology™ workshops as of August 2023. In these workshops, participants learn about the history of gin and the various botanicals and spices that can be used to make gin before creating a bottle custom-tailored to their palate. During COVID-19, Kim offered a GINiology™ at-home program whereby people could answer a questionnaire and then receive a recipe and a bottle of gin based on their answers.

Also, the Karricks worked to help change the liquor laws to permit distilleries to carry products from other producers in their tasting rooms. As per the current law, up to 20 percent of their SKUs (stock-keeping units) can be products from other distilleries. After the founder of Salish Sea Organic Liqueurs sadly passed away and the distillery was not purchased by anyone, Kim decided to carry his products as a way to celebrate and share his work. They also chose some products like Bad Dog Rye and 2BAR Bourbon because they do not make those styles of whiskey.

In Kim's estimation, Edmonds offers many local events that allow businesses like hers to connect and support each other. For example, Kim and four other women business owners launched Edmonds Localvore to encourage people to spend a day in Edmonds shopping, eating and drinking

Distiller Kim Karrick leads a GINiology™ workshop, where she teaches participants how to craft a personalized gin recipe tailored to their specific tastes. *Courtesy of Scratch Distillery.*

at all five of their locations, with special experiences at each location and grand prizes for those who participated and shopped at all.[266] This program was so envied by other businesses in town that the group finally allowed other businesses to participate, though they had to cap it at ten establishments in order to keep it doable and worthwhile for the customers and businesses.[267]

Next, drive east for a tour of **Temple Distilling Company**'s intimate space in neighboring Lynnwood. Cofounder and distiller AJ Temple has been destroying the kitchen since he was about five years old. His love of culinary creation and adventure translated into the cocktail world when he was of drinking age. He's always loved gin because he feels you can really taste all the ingredients that go into it. (In comparison, AJ views whiskey as more like baking, where you start with just a few ingredients and then add in nature and time.)

AJ and his wife, Jamie, began searching for a space within their modest budget that met the extra fire requirements (especially sprinklers) required to operate a distillery. In 2015, they took the plunge after finding a place on Craigslist with about eight hundred square feet that fulfilled their needs. Several years later, the warehouse next to them moved, and they were able to expand their operations. As part of this expansion, they've added

Temple Distilling Company interior. *Photo credit: Temple Distilling Company.*

limoncello and aquavit to their lineup, with the latter a tribute to AJ's half-Swedish roots, and are aging their first bourbon and American single malt. By using small (but not insignificant) percentages of more unique fermentable grains such as oats and local triticale wheat, they aim to make their whiskey more complex when compared to the countless offerings of one or two-note bourbons.

On venturing into the tasting room, you have the sense of entering a quiet, welcoming space akin to a neighborhood bookstore. This literary vibe speaks to the Temples' love of reading, especially when accompanied by a dry martini.

AJ has a particular affinity for the old-world European dry gins made with local ingredients, as well as venturing elsewhere for products like cassia cinnamon bark and juniper berries used in gins that are not local to the Pacific Northwest. Temple Distilling utilizes a custom bain-marie-style pot still that uses indirect oil heating, eliminating hot spots and lending a "slow and low" approach to heating their botanicals, which in turn doesn't destroy the delicate notes often lost in large-scale gin production.

Temple's collaborations with local businesses include barrel-sharing programs with close to half a dozen local breweries, as well as other distillers like Kaiser of 2BAR Spirits, whom he knows from their joint work with the Washington Distillers Guild, where AJ serves as secretary and Kaiser is vice president. Also, Temple Distilling sponsors cocktail competitions among Seattle-area bartenders, with the winning bartender invited to collaborate on a special-release gin with that bartender's name on the bottle.[268]

Then head over east to Maltby, home of **J.P. Trodden Distilling**. The distillery was named after J.P. Trodden, who grew up in north-central Washington in a region called the Okanagan. His father was the very first mail carrier for a mail route called the Star Route, with J.P. taking over the route in the early 1930s. This route crossed back and forth between the U.S. and Canadian borders, with bootleggers transporting spirits along this route, and J.P. stashed a few brown bottles in his mail bag. These spirits were shared among J.P.'s friends in cabin 5, located along the Star Route, which is now owned by owner and distiller Mark Nesheim.

Since the distillery's inception in 2010, Nesheim has been sourcing the corn and winter wheat he grinds for use in his bourbons from a local farmer. Given that bourbon is a spirit unique to the United States, he prides himself on using all American-made equipment, including their copper still from nearby Oregon, glass bottles from Tennessee and new oak barrels. He sells his used barrels to local wineries and breweries, as well as collaborating on some barrel aging and distillation projects. Trodden's community-building events include bourbon and food pairings, cocktail classes, floral design classes, cigar nights, live music and holiday parties.[269]

Travel north to Snohomish for a spirited conversation with John Wohlfert of **Wohlfert Craft Distilling** about how he and his wife continue their respective families' distilling traditions. John's great-grandpa, Johann

This is a 1920s photo of John Wohlfert's great-grandparents in front of their fancy vehicle and one of many homes they acquired from their successful family "baking business." *Courtesy of Wohlfert Craft Distilling.*

Wohlfert, immigrated from Bavaria to New York City in 1890 at the age of just fourteen. He married and opened several successful bakeries, which became a more spirited clandestine operation during Prohibition. As the fermenting yeast and sugar smelled similar to bread, they were able to distill their brews undetected and were even able to downplay a still explosion as simply the result of, say, a gas leak.

John's wife, Karen Mueller (a name given to those who lived in a millhouse) Wohlfert, carries on her ancestors' love of working with grains and developing recipes for baking and beverages. Her family also made spirits during Prohibition.

For years, the couple dreamed of opening a distillery to continue their family tradition, with John looking at stills and Karen developing recipes. In 2018, they formed Wohlfert Craft Distilling on the property where they live, and it opened to the public in 2021. They handcraft their wares from locally sourced grains and the clear water that comes from their underground aquifer. Their signature Starter Sugar Shine contains the secret ingredients that made Great-Grandpa Johann's "bakeries" so successful. The recipes developed by Karen include Spark Basil Vodka and Clutch Coffee Liqueur. Most of their mash is corn-based, which they source from local suppliers, with the remaining ingredients also sourced locally when possible.[270]

Also, be sure to stop by **Skip Rock Distillers**, founded in 2009 by Snohomish natives Ryan and Julie Hembree with a desire to meld their passions for local food and good drinks. They chose the name Skip Rock because they wanted a short name that was easy to remember and had a positive connotation, adding that everyone has good memories of skipping rocks.

Skip Rock's diverse product line affords something for every spirit connoisseur, including fruit liqueurs, gin, rum, whiskey, vodka and a Vivian brandy that begins as Viognier wine from Lupine Vineyards in Manson. Whenever possible, the Hembrees use local grains and fruits, and they've developed relationships with family farmers who produce the highest quality crops for those products not grown in Washington State.

In the beginning, Chris Morris from Woodford Reserve in Versailles, Kentucky, helped the Hembrees learn how to make whiskey. As Skip Rock was one of the first craft distillers in Washington State, the Hembrees found their biggest challenge was convincing consumers and bartenders to try something new instead of relying on their favorite national brands. They found their niche by making all Skip Rock's products from scratch, making better cuts with their whiskeys and paying more attention to detail. In addition, they work with other local distilleries like BROVO Spirits and Temple Distilling to use their spirits in their cocktails. Also, the Hembrees consult with others looking to enter the distillery business to help them develop a well-defined vision of their brand and how they wish to bring it to market.[271]

Woodinville

Next up is a visit to Woodinville. This town situated in the Sammamish Valley has emerged as the heart of an adult beverage renaissance with a growing and thriving winery, microbrewery, distillery and cider culture.

Woodinville Whiskey Company began with best friends Orlin Sorensen and Brett Carlile's dream of making the greatest craft whiskey in the world. Under the mentorship of industry icon David Pickerell, former master distiller for Maker's Mark, they explored how to bring the time-honored traditions of bourbon production into a craft environment. They sought to access the best barrels and coopers in the world and the most technologically advanced distilling equipment, as well as locally sourcing all their grains from the Omlin Family Farm in Quincy, Washington run by third-generation farmers, Arnie and Phyllis Omlin. Their equipment (1,320-gallon handmade pot still, sixteen-plate bubble-cap "Superaromator" rectification column and two dephlegmators for ultra-purification) stands over twenty-five feet tall and produces seven barrels of whiskey per day.[272] In 2017, the distillery was acquired by Moët Hennessy.[273]

BROVO Spirits was founded by Mhairi Voelsgen and Erin Brophy in 2011 with a mission to create the North American vocabulary for traditional European products: amari, aperitivo, liqueurs and vermouth. Their products are all natural, with no artificial colors or flavors, no high fructose corn syrup and no fillers or additives. They are James Beard Foundation nominees for Outstanding Beer, Wine or Spirits producer and winner of the inaugural Alchemist Award from the American Distilling Institute.[274]

COVID-19 hit right as husband-and-wife team Jess and Bing were applying for their liquor license. Hence, the first product they produced at **Copper Cat Distilling** was hand sanitizer that they donated to first responders and essential workers. Currently, they share their passion for creative craft cocktails through events such as their spirit-themed cocktail classes.[275]

When **Puget Sound Rum Company** received its federal Distilled Spirits Plant (DSP) permit and opened its tasting room, it was named Four Leaf Spirits, as it produced two separate brands of spirits under the banners of Four Leaf Spirits and Puget Sound Rum Company, respectively. Since there is no sugarcane grown in Washington State, craft distillers looking to produce spirits made from locally sourced ingredients do not focus on producing rum. Sensing a need for a locally distilled rum, owners Tom and Matt chose to focus their passion and efforts on making rum. So they rebranded their tasting room as Puget Sound Rum Company, though they still produce Four Leaf Spirits products. While many of their raw materials aren't locally sourced, they love using other local barrels to age their spirits and have worked with other distilleries, breweries, cideries and meaderies to make collaborative products.[276]

Northwest Spirits' sister family of restaurants (Von's 1000 Spirits and Sharps Roasthouse) spent a decade infusing and aging spirits in-house. From this venture, they decided to establish a distillery and opened their tasting room to the public in 2022. The founders, the Firnstahls, along with the executive staff have strong roots in the Seattle and Eastside communities,

A beautifully restored barback from the late 1800s adorns Northwest Spirits' tasting room. This barback once belonged to the famous Seattle saloon Jake O'Shaughnessy's, which was one of the many restaurants in the greater Seattle area opened by their founder's family. *Courtesy of Northwest Spirits.*

having been in the local restaurant industry for over fifty years. They chose to establish their distillery in Woodinville as this area attracted a community of spirit producers, which was starting to attract visitors to the area. They found that the local Woodinville Chamber and Wine Country Association welcomed them with open arms and all of their members know and support each other unlike anything they've ever seen.[277]

Pacific Distillery was founded as Marc Bernhard's amateur effort to make absinthe, a hobby he admits got out of control. Once the TTB released a notice allowing distillers and importers to use the term *absinthe* as long as its contents were in line with the FDA's rules in 2007, Bernhard decided to open his distillery in Woodinville that year to take advantage of the foot traffic from those visiting the growing Woodinville boutique winery and craft brewery scene.[278] He also chose to make gin as he loves a well-made gin, as well as adding vodka to the lineup in 2014 after customers began asking for this particular spirit.

As one of the pioneers behind Washington State's craft distillery boom, Bernhard found himself working as a lone wolf, developing his own systems. After helping to form the Washington Distillers Guild in 2008, he observed a greater camaraderie emerge among his fellow distillers. Currently, he's a member of Artisan Hill, a nonprofit organization consisting of Woodinville wineries, breweries and distilleries,[279] as well as forming personal relationships with some of the winemakers where he makes spirits like brandies, port and grappa for them.[280]

After leaving Woodinville, pay a quick visit to **Duvall Distillery** in Duvall. This distillery is the result of mixing decades of experience in all things spirits-related with a mad scientist-esque desire to push the envelope in flavor and taste. As per its website, Duvall Distillery aims to produce vodka, liqueur, grappa and more with an "Old School Cool" feel with pride in bringing a big flavor, higher proof, "Real Deal Hand Crafted Product" to their community, friends and family.[281]

NORTHWEST WASHINGTON

John Lundin describes Everett as a city with great character and grit and the perfect place to build a distillery. "I love how the city captures an intimate connection between a working waterfront and the high cascade crest. We have access to the best water source for our production and get to enjoy the beauty and bustle of the West Coast's largest marina." The idea for **Bluewater Organic Distilling** began onboard an anchored sailboat when Lundin explored a simple distilling experiment that lit the flame for a business. Since its founding in 2008, this distillery has grown to be a community-focused independent distillery and tasting room, along with a retail store, a craft cocktail bar and fresh bistro and a private event venue. The distillers work with hand-hammered direct-fired kettles that carry a legacy stretching back eight centuries. Sustainability is part of Bluewater's culture, and its organic spirits are USDA-certified organic, part of One Percent for the Planet and bottled in American glass.[282]

James Bay Distillers Ltd. began in 2014 when Ernest Troth and his wife, Leigh, created it as a Virginia C corporation. The Troths registered the company in British Columbia in 2016 and moved from the United States to Canada in 2017 to open near Victoria, BC. In 2018, they identified a more advantageous location at Paine Field in Everett and pivoted to return to the United States. The Troths have found a great local community in Everett and Mukilteo and regularly support local chambers of commerce and civic groups in local fundraising efforts.

The Troths source most of their local ingredients throughout the Pacific Northwest, as well as wild harvesting a few items and obtaining the organic kumquats for their gin from California. This commitment to craft can be seen at their distillery, where art from local artists is on display in their tasting room. Also, all their labels feature a float plane logo inspired by the de Havilland Beaver, a Canadian aircraft used by Kenmore Air and others flying from Seattle to British Columbia and Alaska. These labels reflect local history and stories, as do their products, such as their Cadboro organic chocolate–infused whiskey, which honors the *Cadboro*, a notable schooner in Puget Sound owned by the HBC from 1820 to 1864 that now lies just off-shore at Port Angeles. Also, their Strait Up Killer Vodka label displays an orca whale and the Strait of Juan de Fuca.[283]

Up in Edison is **Terramar Brewstillery**, founded in 2019 by the husband-and-wife team of Chris and Jen Barker. According to Chris, "The quirky town of Edison is the ideal place to have a distillery due to its central location in the Skagit Valley for sourcing ingredients. Also, Edison has a thriving art and foodie community." Their speakeasy is a twenty-one-and-over space with a focus on craft cocktails, while their taproom has a more casual family-friendly feel. As head distiller and brewer, Barker views distilling as a natural progression of the process of brewing. In his estimation, "The flavor of a spirit starts with the brewing process. Just like brewing different styles of beer, we brew a spirit wash with the flavors we are trying to achieve in each spirit. To add to the mix, we also make hard cider from locally pressed apples so that we can do brandies and eau de vie."[284]

Further north, in Bellingham, is **Chuckanut Bay Distillery**. Its interior speaks to the history behind this historic building. Built in 1910, this site was home to a JCPenney from the 1930s to the 1960s.[285] Cofounder Kelly Andrews recalls spending five years renovating and refurbishing this building, which included removing over eight hundred thousand pounds of debris.

When possible, cofounder Matt Howell and the rest of his team utilized materials from the original building, especially railings, old timber and steel beams found in the stairs, an adjustable table that moves up and down and the tasting room bar and counter. Also, the former boiler room fire door now divides their tasting room, and reclaimed wood that was burned in a fire long ago and then charred a bit more for uniformity is used throughout the distillery. Other touches include bathroom door handles made from elevator parts, bar and light fixtures crafted from the original building's steel beams and a penny-farthing bike sculpted from reclaimed steel and metal parts.

Top: Bar and penny-farthing bicycle. *Courtesy of Chuckanut Distillery.*

Bottom: JCPenney sign on display. *Courtesy of Chuckanut Distillery.*

Visitors are greeted via a welcome station made from old elevator parts, with the space designed so that customers can view the distillery operation as they dine and drink. Also, the bike that Howell used to grind over thirteen thousand pounds of potatoes for their first vodka is on display in their tasting room. A rooftop bar and large event space that can hold up to three hundred people is in the works.

Given this recycle and repurpose ethos, it's no surprise that sustainability is a priority for this distillery. As an example, a custom-made steel tank holds the spent mash until a local farmer comes to pick it up and give it to their livestock.

Those looking to explore Bellingham's past and present might want to check out Bellinghistory's Good Time Girls, who partner with local businesses including Chuckanut Distillery. In particular, their Sin and Gin tour explores the history of vice from the early saloon days when there was a licensed red-light district and open gambling through the Prohibition years when it all went underground and beyond. They have a version of this tour in Bellingham's historic Fairhaven neighborhood, which was its own town until 1903, when the town of "Bellingham" was born from a merger of Fairhaven and New Whatcom. In researching this tour, co-owner/operator Kolby LaBree was surprised to learn that her great-grandfather was jailed in Bellingham during a Prohibition-era bust for being a rumrunner.[286]

Then head up to Lynden home of **Bellewood Farmstead & Distillery**, which had the distinction of being Washington State's first true "farm-to-glass" apple distillery. They grew the premium-quality fruit that went into their brandy, vodka and gin.[287]

Next travel further north to Arlington for a tour of **Bad Dog Distillery**. Shelly McGlothern describes Bad Dog's distilling process as traditional backwoods distilling. Bad Dog's distillery was built using retrofitted dairy equipment, such as the copper pot still made by Shelly's husband, master distiller Dave, that Bad Dog uses to make its barrel-aged whiskey. The name Bad Dog is the nickname often ascribed to their dog, Hank.[288]

Dave McGlothern started with a tank that was not jacketed. *Courtesy of Bad Dog Distillery.*

Next he cut the top off and added a heat jacket to the bottom. *Courtesy of Bad Dog Distillery.*

Then he made the copper top. *Courtesy of Bad Dog Distillery.*

Everything is heated with hot water, so the still runs low and slow. *Courtesy of Bad Dog Distillery.*

The Northwest leg of this tour concludes in Everson with **Probably Shouldn't Distillery**, founded in 2017 on the Butenschoen's farm, Breckenridge Blueberries. According to Mariah Butenschoen, her husband is a heavy equipment mechanic and was looking for a career change. They had talked about adding value to their farm by finding a creative way to handle their waste fruit. After five years of jumping through hoops, they got the green light and began distilling fruit brandies, followed by a Blueberry Pie Liqueur, Old Tom–style gin and finally a whiskey and a bourbon made with grains from nearby Skagit County.[289]

GREATER SEATTLE (SOUTH)

Now head south of Seattle toward Auburn. Step inside **Blackfish Spirits Distillery** and soak in the historic spirits while savoring their aged straight bourbon and other spirits. Founder and head distiller Mike Gifford traces the spirit of distilling in his family back to 1620, when his ancestor John Gifford was a distiller in London. During Prohibition, his grandparents were both doctors and Quakers who grew juniper on their farm in Maine, which they distilled and sold legally as medicinal liquor. Also, his wife Carrie's grandfather was a moonshiner.

Opposite: Fruit press used to juice fresh cucumbers for small batches of cucumber vodka at Blackfish Spirits Distillery. *Photo credit: Becky Garrison.*

Above: Charcoal sketch of grain in the field hanging above the gin still in Blackfish Spirits Distillery, by Carrie Gifford. *Photo credit: Becky Garrison.*

In 2013, this family-run distillery self-funded its "Harvest to Glass" distillery. Over the next year, the Giffords experienced what they describe as a steep learning curve in obtaining their license. As they waited to open shop, they tested batches on their neighbors. The feedback helped them refine their cooking techniques to produce their spirits, which are all made from Washington-grown harvests.

The term *blackfish* was used by sailors to describe the orca whales that live in Puget Sound. The Giffords chose this name because it captures the adventurous spirit of the Pacific Northwest. Gifford compares the delight and magic they feel when they watch orcas at play with the thrill they experience when they watch their spirits emerge from their stills.[290]

Continue south to Edgewood, home of **Nightside Distillery**, founded by Tom Greene in 2013. The name of the distillery comes from longshore terminology: *nightside* means the night work on the docks. Its spirits are made primarily from local ingredients, such as apple juice from Tree Top in Selah and corn from Toppenish. According to Greene, Nightside creates spirits for "pleasure, perfection and the pride of seeing repeat customers, as well as that smile when they take their first sip and say, 'Oh, my God! That's delicious!'"

Other Pacific Northwest influences appear on Nightside's labels, which feature images of Seattle's skyline and waterfront. Also, one of the pillars of the business is community involvement. To this end, Nightside supports its local fire/police/EMT community, the local food bank, the senior center, the Fair Foundation, Tacoma Arts and the local Edgewood Athletics Little League.[291]

Next up is **Pursuit Distilling Co.** in Enumclaw, where Sam Agnew and his brother-in-law, Tyler Teeple, a home moonshiner, laid down their first barrel in 2017. They dreamed of creating a company that brings people together in celebration of the good times and those to come. This family-owned craft spirits distillery creates high-quality grain-to-glass whiskeys, vodkas and other private-label spirits, with their cold brew whiskey as their flagship spirit. They source all their grain from Small's Family Farm in Walla Walla and utilize local Pacific Northwest resources and sustainable options whenever possible.

In Agnew's estimation, some of their best spirits come from these collaborations with craft breweries. In 2018, they began collaborating with the now-shuttered Portland-based Bridgeport Brewing Company, which offered Agnew and Teeple their beer gratis for distilling purposes as they were going out of business. The following year, they began working with Crux Fermentation Project in Bend, Oregon, to produce a small batch of straight bourbon whiskey. The meticulous wash is customized by Crux's master brewer, Larry Sidor, and the wash is then distilled by Pursuit Distilling Co. and aged for over two years in charred new American oak barrels.[292]

Continuing into Tacoma is **Old Soldier Distillery**, the first craft distillery in this city. It aims to create unique old-fashioned spirits—for example, using a traditional corn whiskey recipe from a distant relative who made this whiskey during the Civil War.[293]

In Lakewood, **Mastrogiannis Distillery & Winery**'s focus on grapes began with Ilias Mastrogiannis's memories of growing up in Greece. His dad was a mason turned winemaker, and the entire family would assist in crushing grapes during harvest. That upbringing, along with the fact that no one in Washington State was making grape brandies of the quality he knew existed, led to Mastrogiannis's decision to start their distillery in 2016 with that singular focus. The winery opened about three years later. In addition to grape brandies, they have a vermouth that's a combination of their rosé wine and their brandy.[294]

Next on the journey is a scenic stop in Kitsap Peninsula, a bedrock community of Seattle that encompasses thirty-two eclectic communities surrounded by over three hundred miles of saltwater shoreline. Here is the distribution center, administrative offices, and tasting room for **Heritage**

Distilling Company Inc.® (**HDC**) in Gig Harbor. It first came to market in 2011 with its current line of spirits, including a line of canned cocktails; Cocoa Bomb Chocolate Whiskey; its Elk Rider® series; the HDC series, featuring more than twenty naturally flavored vodkas; the Batch No. 12® line of spirits; Florescence (a partnership with Danielle Kartes and Rustic Joyful Food); Stiefel's Select premium whiskeys; Spirits Advent Calendar; and more. Since opening its initial distillery in Gig Harbor, HDC now has full-scale production facilities and tasting rooms in the Craft District in Tumwater and Eugene, Oregon, along with a tasting room in Rosyln. HDC is an active member of the community, helping to raise money for various charities and nonprofit groups across the Pacific Northwest. The company's philanthropic efforts were rewarded with the secretary of state's Corporations for Community award for the state of Washington in 2015 and the Manufacturer of the Year award from the Association of Washington Businesses in 2017.[295]

Then check out **Black Ring Spirits**, located in Port Orchard. Tom and Heather Martin describe their small craft distillery, established in 2018, as operating very much like eighteenth-century small farm distilleries. They use local grains and fruit to make liquor in small batches, with the liquor changing depending on the crops that are in season. Hence, every trip to their tasting room will result in sampling a slightly different array of spirits. Also, they distill and bottle a house whiskey for the Whiskey Gulch CoffeePub, also located in Port Orchard.[296]

Continue south to University Place, home of **Chambers Bay Distilling**. Since producing its first whiskey in 2014, this distillery has drawn inspiration from Puget Sound to create extraordinary spirits with a focus on bourbon.[297]

Over in Tumwater, be sure to pay a visit to **Percival Creek**'s tasting room situated in Tumwater's Craft District. Here visitors can sample beer, cider and spirits made by the next generation of brewers and distillers. Percival Creek products are produced by students and professional staff at South Puget Sound Community College's campus with locally sourced ingredients.[298]

Also in Tumwater **Olympia Distilling Co. & Shoebox Spirits** distributes Olympia Artesian Vodka, along with a new orange-flavored Olympia Vodka, throughout Washington, Oregon, California and Idaho. It also produces several small-batch gins, including Oly Gin, Kelsey Blue Gin and Kelsey Gold Gin. The Kelsey gins are a tribute to a family member they recently lost to cancer. Proceeds from each bottle go to cancer research and Kelsey's two young daughters. Ray Watson and Lesa Givens are the owners and full-time operators of the distillery.[299]

SOUTHWEST WASHINGTON

Drive down to Tenino for a visit to John Bourdon's thirteen-acre farm, where he built **Sandstone Distillery**. When asked how long he's been distilling, Bourdon answers, "Legally?" (Always good for a giggle). The actual answer is that Bourdon's been a legal distiller for nine years as of this writing, though he's been distilling for over twenty years.

The grains for Bourdon's spirits are grown just forty-five minutes away on his cousin's farm in Lewis County, and he obtains other ingredients via foraging, farmers markets and other local sources. Also, he trades used barrels with area brewers: the brewers use them to age their beers, then Bourdon uses them to finish his whiskeys.

Bourdon starts and finishes Sandstone's spirits with fresh, clean Pacific Northwest water drawn straight from the earth at their estate distillery. Their more unique spirits include WTF ("What's the Finish") Gin, that's two-year barrel aged in a whiskey barrel that, as per their website, "subsequently aged a double-hopped citrus IPA from Top Rung Brewery in nearby Lacey"; Stone Carver Bacon Whiskey, a bacon-infused whiskey using the bacon from the hogs that ate the spent grains that went into making their White Whiskey;

Gabe (*behind*) is a 1,600-gallon "milk condensing machine" built in 1920 by the Arthur Harris Co. that was converted to a bourbon still. Distillers John (*left*) and his son Justin (*right*) stand beside Rafael, their twenty-plate vodka column. *Courtesy of Sandstone Distillery.*

Left: They went "pro" with these sixty-gallon soup kettles repurposed from navy surplus. Hark (*left*) produces both of Sandstone's Gins, and Harold (*right*) makes the award-winning White Whiskey, which is also the base spirit for their Bacon Whiskey. *Courtesy of Sandstone Distillery.*

Right: From humble beginnings experimenting with mash bills, this little five-gallon still consists of two stainless steel milk buckets welded together with a column slapped on top and was the second step in the theme of retrofitting and reusing materials to create unique spirits. *Courtesy of Sandstone Distillery.*

Andrew's Hammer, a high-proof whiskey made in honor of stone carver and adventurer Andrew Wilson, whose hammer symbolizes the can-do spirit of Sandstone Distillery; and their Coffee Liqueur, made in partnership with local coffee roasters Batdorf & Bronson. In addition, distillery co-owner Jenni Bourdon created Wild Heart Sipping Vinegars as a complex and delicious component of their signature craft cocktails. These vinegars are made using the lessons they learned from slowly aging their spirits, which allows them to reach the perfect equilibrium between the tangy apple cider vinegar, fresh fruit juices and savory herbs and spices.[300]

Over in the Chehalis River Valley in Rochester is the home of **Talking Cedar Brewery and Distillery**, a tribally owned and operated thirty-five-thousand-square-foot craft brewery, distillery, tasting room and restaurant that has the distinction of being the first tribally owned distillery built on tribal land. The Chehalis Tribe and HDC formed a partnership where they successfully lobbied Congress in 2018 to repeal the Indian Intercourse Act of 1834, which prohibited distilling on Native tribal lands.

The name Talking Cedar speaks to the significance of the cedar tree in the tribe's past, as well as serving as an important symbol in the Pacific Northwest. Other regional influences include working with local farmers to develop the best wheat and barley varieties for this region. In addition, they forage the botanicals used in their gin, which include spruce tips, black fennel and Nootka rose. Also, they recently partnered with Copperworks to help them scale by handling all their farm-specific malts in a manner that enables Copperworks to increase its production significantly while still adhering to its high-quality controls.[301]

The next stop is Centralia to check out **King Distillery**, whose tagline claims, "It's good to be king." King Distillery's one mission is to create great products at a great price. Its first product, King V vodka, is now on the market, with other products to come.[302]

Head down to Battleground and embark on a historical take on distilling with James Schefers, owner and founder of **Battle Crest Distillary**. He spent forty years in Alaska, where he did some distilling. Also, his father was a dairy farmer in Minnesota, where he grew Minnesota 13—Schefers adds that Al Capone procured whiskey made from this corn variety from Stearns County, Minnesota. In the 1930s, Schefers's father got into the distilling business along with many other farmers in Stearns County, with his brother-in-law getting arrested for running alcohol and being sent to Fort Leavenworth, Kansas, for a year.

Given this family history, it's no surprise that all the stories on Battle Crest's product labels deal with historical facts about real-life people and events. Their first product was a vodka based on their family's farming history in Germany that goes back over five hundred years. Four of their five current products center on their ancestors and parents, who were either involved in the making of spirits or pioneers of cultural elements used in their spirits. For example, the name of their rye, Petticoat Courage, isn't associated with their family history but denotes the story of how Battle Ground got its name and how Captain Strong of Fort Vancouver received a red petticoat as his badge of courage for his failure to bring in the local Indians during the Yakima uprising Also, their coffee liqueur, named Kanada Foster's Coffee Ridge, tells his wife Audrey's third-great-grandfather's story. He was a pioneer of East Tennessee and was the first to bring coffee into the area. His property became known as Coffee Ridge, with its gristmill on display at the Tennessee State Museum of History.

Battle Crest's distillery tours get into the nitty-gritty of how it makes its products from scratch. James estimates that about 90 percent of the distillery's ingredients come from Washington State. Its grain is ground on Scheferfield Farm, where its farm craft distillery is located. Battle Crest source its corn, barley, rye and other grains from a farmer in Quincy who grows all his corn for distillation purposes and its malted grains from the Country Malt Group in Vancouver.[303]

As Vancouver's first craft distillery since the HBC closed shop in 1836, **Quartz Mountain Distillers** has been in operation since 2020. It is family-owned and operated with a legacy rooted in wilderness, adventure and laid-back gatherings.[304]

Moving west to Stevenson, one finds another family-owned distillery, **Skunk Brothers Spirits**. It was started by a family of disabled veterans who derived their name from their pops, Skunk. He earned his nickname when he ran into a skunk during a snowstorm. Skunk's father was a moonshiner in Oregon, and they're here to go legal with the family business.[305]

The Islands

Take a break from the stress of traveling up and down I-5 and soak up the small-town ambiance and maritime culture of Washington State's coastal distilleries.

Bainbridge Island

First stop is Bainbridge Island, a short ferry ride from Seattle and a haven for those who appreciate the fine art of distilling and whiskey in particular.

Founded in 2008 by Keith Barnes, a distilled spirits branding and marketing expert with over thirty-five years of experience in the field. **Bainbridge Organic Distillers** is one of the few distilleries surrounded completely by open saltwater. This unique microclimate is fueled by sun-drenched days and a brine-marine air that seeps into the distillery's charred American white oak barrels as they age, adding subtlety and nuance to their organic whiskeys, vodka and gin. From selecting USDA organic grains grown by brothers Tom and Ray Williams on a parcel of land in Walla Walla County once owned by the HBC to using waters drawn from deep aquifers whose source is the coastal Olympic Mountain Range, they seek to create spirits distilled old-school style while also embracing the most modern organic technology on the market.

In 2012, Barnes started the distillery's Mizunara oak (*Quercus crispula*) project after learning about efforts being organized to preserve the Yama site, where Japanese immigrants lived on Bainbridge Island from 1883 to 1922. He began the seemingly herculean task of importing Mizunara oak slabs purchased at the annual Mizunara auction in Hokkaido, Japan, and then having Gibbs Brothers Cooperage, a small family-owned barrel maker in Arkansas, craft finished whiskey barrels from this rare wood. According to Barnes, even under the best of conditions, Mizunara oak can be rather finicky. It's very porous, which results in frequent leaks and a high percentage of evaporation when it's made into barrels. The wood is also brittle, making fashioning it into barrels at all quite a chore.[306] These virgin barrels were filled with a single-grain whiskey, double distilled from unmalted Full Pint and Alba barley grown in Washington State's Skagit Valley.

Four years later, they released two hundred bottles of Bainbridge Yama Single Mizunara Cask Whiskey, which has the distinction of being the first non-Japanese whiskey aged exclusively in virgin Japanese Mizunara casks. A future release will age longer, with some barrels receiving a second fill. According to *Whisky Advocate*, which awarded Yama the 2016 Craft Whiskey of the Year award, "Yama expands the palette of American whiskey, is a testament to the determination of the distiller, gives back to the community, and delights the whiskey lover with new flavors. It fulfills what great whiskey can accomplish in making the world a better place."[307]

Profits from the sale of Bainbridge Yama Mizunara Cask Single Grain Whiskey will support the ongoing efforts to preserve the unique Yama history for the study and enrichment of generations to come.[308] Currently, Bainbridge

Bainbridge Yama Mizunara Cask Single Grain Whiskey. *Photo credit: ian@iancoble.com.*

Organic Distillers remains one of the only distilleries outside of Japan with a dedicated virgin Japanese Mizunara oak barrel maturation program.

While Bainbridge Organic Distillers has the distinction of being Bainbridge Island's first legal distillery, as Barnes observes, they're not the first ones to distill on this island. Back in the 1860s through the early 1900s, the Whiskey Forty Saloon, located adjacent to the dry mill town of Port Madison on Bainbridge Island, served thirsty timber mill workers frontier spirits made by an Irishman. Apparently, this nineteenth-century distiller jumped ship, swam to the island and set up his still nearby. Barnes paid homage to this infamous saloon by naming his first bourbon the Whiskey Forty Saloon Organic Bourbon. Other historical touches found throughout the distillery include Barnes's vast collection of more than four hundred bottles of whiskey, vodka and gin distilled prior to 1960.[309]

Before leaving Bainbridge Island, be sure to stop by **Highside Distilling** for another taste of island-based spirits. After incorporating Highside Distilling LLC in late 2015, Matt, Helen, and Jeff Glenn received their DSP permit in September 2017 and sold their first bottle of gin on November 17, 2018.

Their island location and maritime climate are important to them in seeking to create an American single malt whiskey that is inspired by traditional Scottish styles while exerting the influence of the Pacific Northwest to make this whiskey uniquely their own. All the malted barley used for their American single malt whiskey is grown in-state and sourced from a variety of local craft malters.

Along those lines, their gin and Italian-inspired amari are made from a base of 100 percent Washington-grown apples. Their amari is then macerated with a combination of traditional and local botanicals, including Cascade hops, coffee and honey. Their proximity to great native ingredients on the Kitsap and Olympic Peninsulas helps to influence the flavor profiles of their seasonal gins and botanical liqueurs, such as local Bainbridge Island walnuts, fir and spruce tips and Olympic Peninsula Aronia berries, along with engaging the local herbalist community to grow botanicals like Chinese rhubarb root that are not native to this area.[310]

San Juan Islands

For those embarking on the ferry heading to the San Juan Islands, Wheelhouse Distillery in Anacortes offered an experiential journey into Washington State's Prohibition past. As per Wheelhouse's now shuttered website, antique Prohibition-era pieces adorned its tasting room, including an old still, a tasting cup purchased in Eastern Washington and historical pictures from the local museum on the wall depicting Skagit County events and bars. Mabel the Whiskey Runner, a 1931 Dodge Brothers four-door sedan, was moved to the distillery for restoration, with plans for her to be the ultimate whiskey-advertising vehicle when fully restored.[311]

Since launching in 2014, **Orcas Island Distillery** in the town of Eastsound on Orcas Island has been on a mission to resurrect delightful spirits whose flavors have almost disappeared from the American palate. Its apple brandy is made from fruit hand-picked in the heirloom orchards of the San Juan Islands. Also, farmers in the Skagit Valley grow the organic grains that form the basis of their single malt whiskey and genever gins. In addition, their aged spirits begin in new American oak and are finished in rye whiskey or cognac barrels.[312]

San Juan Island Distillery was founded in 2011 at the existing location of Westcott Bay Cider in Roche Island on San Juan Island. The distillery's place begins with the apples from an orchard two hundred yards away that are used for its cider and the base spirit for almost all its spirits. Currently, the distillery makes fourteen different gins, several liqueurs and brandies using ingredients that are either foraged or grown locally by its owner Suzy's sister. One exception is its lavender, which comes from nearby Pelindaba Lavender Farm. Other collaborations include a Siegerrebe Brandy with wine from Lopez Island Vineyards and a whiskey with beer from San Juan Island Brewing Co. Also, San Juan Island Distillery does contract distilling for Lopez Island Vineyards and for Madrone Winery, whose wintes they fortify for port.[313]

Whidbey Island

In 2010, Bev and Steve Heising opened **Whidbey Island Distillery** in Langley, where their first product was Loganberry Liqueur, made from a berry with a rich island history. Later, they added raspberry, blackberry and boysenberry to their liqueur production. Often, they trade wine and then give back neutral grape spirits for wineries to use in their production of fortified dessert wines and ports. Then they add their portion of the spirits to Washington-grown berries harvested from Graysmarsh Farm in Sequim to produce their berry liqueurs. Also, they make a rye whiskey with a mash bill of 51 percent Northwest rye and 49 percent barley grown on

Whidbey Island, which they age using traditional barrel aging as well as a nontraditional oak aging that uses oak staves.

After realizing that the workload and cost of labor to produce spirits in a batch-mode still was unsustainable, Steve knew he needed to switch to a continuous still. As the cost of a commercial still proved to be prohibitive, Steve designed and fabricated a prototype still that could meet their needs. He connected a supply of wine to the still and began the heating process. A pure and crisp neutral grape spirit emerged through the parrot within minutes at 190 proof, and the Heising-330 was born. Since then, their continuous stills have been running for tens of thousands of hours and have produced thousands of bottles of spirits.[314]

When **Cultus Bay Distillery** in Clinton opened its doors in 2015, owner Kathy Parks established herself as one of the pioneering female distillers in Washington State. Inside this former boathouse, visitors are invited to take a private tour where Parks shows the stills she made and the work it takes to produce a fine small batch of craft bitters and spirits. Her unique spirits include Poitin (Gaelic for "little pot"), a local spirit made by Celts when law enforcement wasn't looking. This spirit is a high-proof white triple-pot-stilled single malt whiskey that's malty, strong and white. Also, she makes Mulligan, an essentially civilized Poitin that starts with a grain bill, with its caramel and honey grain notes enhanced by the soft tannin flavors from once-used bourbon barrel oak barrels that were cleaned and re-heat-treated to emphasize a different flavor profile from its bourbon origins.[315]

Long Beach Peninsula

In 2017, **Adrift Distillers** was started in Long Beach by Matt Lessnau, Adrift Distillers' head distiller, and Tiffany and Brady Turner, owners of Adrift Hospitality. They wanted to offer a unique and engaging experience for guests of the Adrift Hotel and their other nearby properties. Their range of spirits includes vodka, gin, whiskey, aquavit and popular liqueurs. From their geographic location just steps from the beach and surrounding agriculture to their collaborative partners, they keep their spirits as locally inspired as possible and use their spirits to highlight the best of the region. The 100 percent Washington-grown grain, cranberries and rhubarb they use are grown just five miles away, and their bourbon uses grain grown both in the Skagit Valley and the Palouse.

From the beginning, they partnered with other local businesses to create some hyper-local unique spirits for their customers. They accomplish this

Adrift Distillers' exterior. *Photo credit: Sage Quigley.*

through their Collaborative Spirits Series, where they work with local purveyors, farmers, roasters and brewers to create something that both parties are proud of and make connections that bridge local industries.[316]

OLYMPIC PENINSULA

Next, take a drive around Olympic Peninsula, a region anchored by the Olympic National Park and bordered by the Hood Canal, the Pacific Ocean and Strait of Juan de Fuca.

First stop is Aberdeen for a visit to **Westport Winery Garden Resort** and **Ocean's Daughter Distillery**, which co-owner Kim Roberts describes as "a winery with spirits for those who just don't dig wine." Currently, they offer thirty different wines plus thirty different spirits, so the list is extensive on both sides. In Roberts's estimation, this gives their guests lots of choices every day and reasons to visit on multiple trips. She finds these products go well together, and they serve them in their restaurant as well. Their most popular spirit is their Purple Reign lavender lemon gin, with their Single Malt Barrel Ride as their top whiskey; their top liqueur is Morgans, a chocolate chip mint cream. As the 2022 Washington Winery of the Year from *Great Northwest Wine Magazine*, they view themselves as outliers in the wine industry since they are so far from any other wineries, yet they are making big award winners.[317] Roberts finds this to be much the same with the distillery, as they operate in their own remote bubble with dedicated fans that share their enthusiasm for their products with family and friends.[318]

Port Angeles Distilling Company was founded by Cynthia Malane in 2014. She was encouraged by her late husband, Ryan, to follow her dream to become part of the distilling community. Her background in technology and research was a perfect match for her interest in starting a distillery. Her general love of cooking, flavors and the science behind mysteries in the kitchen, plus her patience and curiosity, led to products such as their 14 Knots Vodka and 14 Knots Gin. Both are blends of local Washington apples, pears and grapes, with the inclusion of juniper in the gin product. Also, Catitude, a blend in memory of the Malanes' beloved cat, Andorra, has the same base as 14 Knots but is also infused with pear, blackberry and fig flavors. When possible, she sources the juice locally as well as bringing the bulk juice over the Cascades.

Until his unfortunate death in 2022, Ryan was more than just an encouraging husband and co-owner of the Coho Ferry of the Blackball Ferry Line. He was a marketing guru, and his touch can be felt throughout this project, such as naming their vodka and gin 14 Knots because of the ferry's history of traveling at fourteen knots. Also during the pandemic, Cynthia received a call to help the first responder community with the hand sanitizer shortage. Gallons of hand sanitizer made their way from Port Angeles to Forks on the peninsula and the Greater Seattle region.[319]

Also in Port Angeles is **Caudill Bros. Distillers**, which was founded in 2017 by Mike Caudill and his brother. Mike was a local building contractor, and they converted his old office into the distillery and tasting room. They began production in 2019 and opened their tasting room in 2021.

The Caudill brothers inherited their distilling chops from their father, Jim, who started Golden Spirits on Samish Island with his partner, Bob Stillnovich. (They were one of the first licensed craft distilleries in Washington State, though the distillery was sold after Jim passed away a few years ago.) All the grains for their American single malt, straight rye whiskey and bourbon are mashed and sourced from Washington State. Also, their brandy from red wine comes from Camaraderie Cellars in Port Angeles, and their apple brandy hails from Finnriver Farm & Cidery in Chimacum.[320]

Incorporated in 2011, **Admiralty Distillers** in Port Townsend has the distinction of being the first legal craft distillery established on the Olympic Peninsula. Founder Jake Soule creates spirits using water from the Olympic

Mountains and local ingredients for flavors and aromas reflective of the Quimper Peninsula, along with collaborations with local wineries, cideries and breweries. When possible, they strive to support other small businesses and minimize their impact on the environment.

Admiralty's current lineup of brandies includes eau de vie; an un-aged fruit brandy made with apples picked from its neighbors' trees and pears grown on local orchards; a marc brandy styled after classic Italian grappa using pomace from premium local winemakers; and a brandy made with uncommon orange muscat grapes and other select Washington-grown varietals. Also, Admiralty makes a Pennant Gin that, as noted on the distillery's website, was "inspired by the Gin Pennant that was originally hoisted around the 1940s as an invitation from one navel ship to another for officers to come aboard for a ration of gin." Grapes are the base for this gin, with the slight sweetness and fruit flavor accentuating the juniper and savory spices, which are balanced with two types of citrus and a hint of locally grown lavender.[321]

Hardware Distillery Co. in Hoodsport is named after the old hardware store built in the 1930s that once inhabited this building. Jan and Chuck Morris purchased the building in 2011 to fulfill their retirement dream of owning a distillery and opened the following year. Touches of Jan's creative spirit are on display throughout the distillery, from the hardware items that adorn the walls to her artwork on their bottles.

Their water flows to them from the Hood Canal Watershed in the next-door Olympic National Forest, and they use grains and fruit grown in Washington State. Currently, they're one of the few U.S. distilleries making a distilled mead (melomel). Their range of Bee's Knees® products is made from 80 percent wildflower honey from Washington beehives and 20 percent local fruit and then distilled to the point where it's no longer a mead. This distilled spirit rests for about three years in new white American oak barrels with a medium char. Also, they collaborate with local businesses like Hoodsport Coffee Co. and Potlatch Brewing Co. in creating their spirits. Other recent projects include a whiskey made from barley that has been malted with peat that comes from a peat bog near the distillery.[322]

CENTRAL AND EASTERN WASHINGTON

Time to head toward the Cascades. First stop, Sultan for a visit to **Curtson Distillery**, an artisan distillery that creates unique specialty spirits based on their passion for aging spirits.[323] Then, over in nearby Leavenworth is **Blue Spirits Distilling**. The name comes from the pure blue waters of nearby Lake Chelan, "a fifty five mile long geological crevice filled with pristine water...originally carved by glaciers." From this water, they produce gin, vodka, whiskey, tequila and Peirates Rum.[324]

Be sure to stop by Rosyln for a quick visit to the **Brick Saloon**.[325] It touts itself as the oldest saloon in Washington, dating to 1889, when John Buffo and Peter Giovanni opened a saloon the same year Washington State achieved statehood. The wooden bar where loggers, coal miners and others have bellied up for a drink through the years was made in England and brought to Portland by way of Cape Horn. During Prohibition, a tunnel in the basement enabled moonshiners to discretely deliver alcohol. According to some accounts, the basement's jail cells served as the city's drunk tank, with jail scenes in the 1979 film *The Runner Stumbles* filmed in these cells. In other Hollywood highlights, this saloon was the watering hole of TV's *Northern Exposure*.

Another original and unique feature is the running water spittoon beneath the bar. Instead of the traditional brass spittoons used by tobacco chewers to spit their juice, the Brick has a twenty-three-foot-long gutter

The Brick Saloon. *Courtesy of the State of Washington Tourism.*

at the foot of the bar, where a stream of water flushes the spit away. In recent years, this gutter has been used for annual "spittoon races," where homemade toy boats are raced the length of the bar. Think a Cub Scout rain-gutter regatta but with tiny boats, cash prizes and alcohol.[326]

Next stop is **Elk Heights Distillery** in Ellensburg. It uses low-volume pot stills to produce small batches of distilled spirits such as whiskey, brandy and rum.[327]

Head just west of Yakima up to Naches Heights for a tour of **Wilridge Vineyard, Winery & Distillery**, described by owner Paul Beveridge as the "Greenest Winery in Washington State." Solar powered, certified organic and certified Biodynamic, refillable bottles—anything Beveridge can do to be more green, he'll do. This includes lobbying the Washington State Legislature to amend the alcohol laws to allow wineries, cideries and breweries to also hold a distilling license—which allows him to produce Grappa and Marc from the pomace of his wine grapes instead of returning it to the vineyard for composting.

Currently, Beveridge produces fine brandy, grappa and other spirits from the grapes, apples, pears, plums, apricots and other fruits grown organically and biodynamically on Wilridge Estate Vineyard and Orchard. These spirits are distilled a single time through an eighty-gallon Portuguese hand-

Wilridge Distillery Tasting Room exterior. *Courtesy of Wilridge Vineyard Winery & Distillery.*

hammered copper alembic pot still made by one of the only two remaining artisans who make traditional stills in this manner. A box of fruit goes into each brandy with no other ingredients added. A growing portion of brandy is aged in French oak barrels.

In addition to tasting his wines and spirits at the Wilridge Estate Vineyard & Farmhouse, those in Greater Seattle can sample Beveridge's wares at Wilridge Pie Wine Bar in Woodinville and in Seattle at Pike Place Market and the original winery in the Madrona neighborhood of Seattle. (While this is a book on distilling, it's telling to note that Beveridge was the first winemaker to set up shop in Seattle in 1988.)[328]

In downtown Yakima, grab a drink at the **Distillarium**, a distillery and bar founded to address what founders Ken and Isabel Miller perceived as a distinct lack of aged Washington spirits on the market. They wanted to bring aged spirits to Washington in a way that utilized the rich grains, fruit and corn that central Washington is known for producing. They began their aging process in 2017, with all their spirits aging for three or four years, depending on the spirit.

While COVID-19 delayed the opening of their tasting room, they were able to finally open in July 2021. They noticed distilleries don't seem to have the same community feel found in wineries and breweries. So they decided

The Distillarium Tasting Room. *Photo credit: Digital Vendetta.*

to add a full kitchen and outdoor patio to their distillery, noting that food can pair well with their aged spirits.[329]

Before leaving Yakima, be sure to pay a visit to **Swede Hill Distilling**, named after the Swede Hill area where the distillery is located. This nickname dates to the early 1900s, when hundreds of Swedish immigrants came to the Yakima Valley and planted orchards in the area. In 2013, Kevin and Pamela Milford founded this distillery in true farm-to-bottle fashion, as Pamela's grandparents were among those early immigrants who planted and farmed the land where the distillery currently resides. Their spirits include moonshine and single-barrel American whiskey.[330]

Continue the journey for a visit to **Vitis Spirits** in Zillah. The dream for this distillery began in 1970 when Celeste Larenas met Sal Leone when she was a foreign exchange student from Chile spending her senior year at Santa Clara High School in California. They reconnected forty-one years later and discovered they both had a passion for wine. Sal started Silver Lake Winery in 1987 and owned a vineyard in Zillah, Washington State, while Celeste's father owned a vineyard in Talca, Chile. When they toured their countries' respective wine regions, Sal learned about the Chilean drink pisco, an ancient spirit made from grapes.

When the Woodinville Whiskey Company sold their equipment and moved to a new facility in 2013, Sal and Celeste decided to purchase their equipment and in 2014 opened the doors of Grapeworks Distilling, located in Woodinville. They continue to operate as Grapeworks Distilling, selling under the brand name Vitis Spirits in Zillah. In addition to pisco, they distill vodka and brandy, with a tasting room at Roza Estates Wine & Spirits.[331]

Then take a quick stop at the **Bluebird Inn** in Bickleton, which also advertises itself as the oldest operating tavern in the state. This building was constructed by Jacob N. Jensen for C.E. Flower and Doctor Hamilton Blair as a drugstore and dwelling in the spring of 1887 and became a saloon that fall. Since this time, there have been many owners of the Bluebird Inn, and it has operated under several different names, which is why some consider the Brick Saloon, to be older as its name has remained consistent throughout the centuries.[332]

Continue to Prosser for a visit to **Monson Ranch Distillery**. Officially launched in 2023, this distillery is led by the third and fourth generations of Monson ranchers, together with master distiller Brian Morton, to create uniquely crafted spirits. Starting with cattle feedlots, the foundation of Monson Ranch was built in the 1930s with the family climbing its way up in the Washington agriculture community as farmers, ranchers and winemakers. With vineyards, orchards and new rye and corn plantings at the family's home ranch in Goose Gap and a state-of-the-art distillery in eastern Washington, Monson Ranch Distillers controls every step of the process for a complete farm-to-bottle experience.[333]

Next up is a stop at **Black Heron**, a boutique winery and distillery in West Richland "dedicated to the handcrafting of fine wines and spirits.[334]

Then head over to Richland for a visit to **Solar Spirits**, a distillery that seeks to put the power of the sun in every bottle. As part of this mission, it utilizes advances in solar technology to generate electricity. For example, the distillery's mash process is powered by solar tubes, and it installed a solar thermal system with the goal of creating a distillery powered entirely by the sun. To bridge the gap, the distillery is purchasing Renewable Energy Credits (REC) to offset its purchased electricity. In addition to sourcing its ingredients directly from Pacific Northwest farms, it works with a local coffee roaster to roast coffee beans for its coffee vodka. In lieu of sugar, the distillery sweetens its spirits with Northwest beet. Its other spirits include several gins, vodkas, cranberry brandy, Cosmic Cosmo (a ready-made cosmopolitan) and a passion project to make a single malt whiskey.[335]

Next up is a visit to Walla Walla, home to world-class wineries and a growing distillery culture. In keeping with the spirit of the region, **2nd Street Distillery**'s tasting room has an old-time theme featuring four whiskeys: Cowboy Bourbon, RJ Callaghan Single Malt, PV Schiro Apple Flavored Whiskey and Reser's Rye Whiskey. The latter spirit is named after W.P. Reser, the first U.S. senator from Washington after Washington became a state in 1889. He established a homestead in Walla Walla in 1865, and his family continues to farm that homestead. Other hand-crafted spirits include vodkas, gins and liqueurs, with their RB Pepper & Garlic Vodka as their best-selling spirit.[336]

Also in Walla Walla, **DW Distilling**, housed in a World War II Army Air Force barracks, showcases many historic artifacts from the base in its tasting room, the Officers' Club. It produces craft brandy from fine Walla Walla wines that are already barrel-aged and bottle-ready. It distills the wines once and then ages them in American oak until they're ready to bottle.[337] Another Walla Walla–based distillery, **Cedar Rain Spirits**, is a family-owned distillery that serves cocktails, beer and samples of their vodkas and liqueurs. Its distiller made a coffee-based liqueur for family gatherings for over three decades before launching Cedar Rain Spirits in December 2019.[338]

Finally, there's **Shot in the Dark Craft Distillery**. This handcrafted, small-batch whiskey distillery focuses on making moonshine with names like

Apple Pie Moonshine, Blind Dog Moonshine (named after Kevin's own blind dog, Phoenix), along with Prohibition Moonshine (80 proof) and Prohibition 101 Moonshine (101 proof), both of which are aged in French oak. Also, it has an 80 proof corn vodka called CornStar.[339]

Then travel toward Spokane for a visit to **Browne Family Spirits**. While Browne Family Vineyards is known for their Walla Walla wines, this family-owned winery launched the Browne Family Spirits Collection in 2022. This collection focuses on locally sourced, limited-edition bourbon, rye and whiskey by Kentucky native master distiller Aaron Kleinhelter, along with gin and vodka. Browne Family's rye, wheat and corn are sourced and milled in nearby Colfax and Ritzville, while the malted rye is sourced from Country Malt, located just down the road from the distillery. Also, the Browne Family Vineyard's tasting rooms in Bellevue and Tacoma carry Browne Family Spirits.[340]

While in Spokane, be sure to pay a visit to **Dry Fly Distilling**, referenced in the "Legislating Liquor" chapter.

The final stop on this spirited statewide road trip is **2 Loons Distillery** in Loon Lake, north of Spokane, founded in 2014 by Greg and Trish Schwartz, two admittedly "slightly loony" craft distillers. They fell in love with the art of distilling after participating in a local distiller's bottling party. They distill their products on their small-scale thirty-gallon still using primarily Washington-grown corn, malted barley and wine, and many of their flavored products include Washington-grown fruits and herbs. They sell their products out of their tasting room and the local bar and grill, as well as doing deliveries throughout Washington several times a year.[341]

As with any road trip, before embarking on a journey to visit any distilleries in person, check out their website or social media profiles to verify their hours of operation, location and other pertinent details.

Chapter 7

THE FUTURE OF DISTILLING

By the time you're holding this book in your hands, odds are the exact number of distilleries listed therein will have shifted. At least one will most likely have shuttered its doors or consolidated its operations, while other aspiring distillers will have emerged to make their mark in the Washington State distillery scene. Such is the nature of the craft distilling industry.

The question remains: How will all these distilleries not only survive but also thrive in a state with some of the highest liquor taxes and regulations in the United States? Poffenroth notes, "I think COVID-19 decimated small distilling in Washington State. A few distillers will become bigger, mostly via the support of a larger owner. Some may consolidate seeking collective efficiency or horsepower, and some will sadly fade away. This is a difficult business, nothing like small brewery or winery projects."[342]

While I experience a far more welcoming, community-minded spirit at a distillery tasting room than in a typical church, I remain struck by who is not at the table. For example, when I initially outlined this book, I included a chapter on women in distilling. After all, as I noted at the start of this book, women functioned as home distillers during colonial times. Also, I learned about some female moonshiners operating during Prohibition, though I only had permission to tell two of these stories. But there simply are not enough female distillers in Washington State to make a full chapter a reality at this juncture.

Similarly, Talking Cedar Brewery and Distillery remains the only distillery run by people of color. Here, it must be noted that these omissions are not

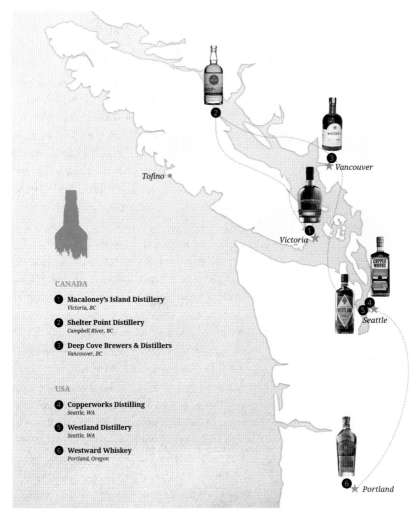

Map of the Northwest Whiskey Trail as of August 2023. *Courtesy of Northwest Whiskey Trail.*

confined to the Pacific Northwest by any means. A range of programs, organizations and scholarships have to emerge on the national level to address these gaps.[343]

Along those lines, in researching this book, I was struck by how many stories remain untold, especially those accounts pertaining to the more illicit aspects of the distilling industry and the saloon culture. In particular, the accounts of how liquor impacted women, children, Native people and freed slaves remain largely unreported, with many of their descendants only willing to chat off the record, if at all. Hopefully, someday these stories can come to light.

What does ring loud and clear is the increasing demand throughout the Pacific Northwest for craft over commercial. Barnes keenly observes, "The market here is excited about local products. I think really good local products will have longevity."[344] As evidence of this interest in purchasing products made via organic and sustainable means, a growing number of distillers have begun experimenting with non-commodity grains and sourcing locally produced fruits, botanicals and other items for their spirits.

This passion for locally sourced sustainable products extends to the proliferation of locally owned bars and restaurants throughout the Pacific Northwest, with far fewer national chain outfits when compared to the strip mall culture that dominates much of the American landscape. In all but the diviest bars, one can order a cocktail made with a spirit distilled in Washington State. Even convenience stores carry a semi-decent array of craft spirits along with beer, cider, hard seltzer and wine.

Recent ventures such as the Northwest Whiskey Trail, which highlights those Northwest coastal distilleries that produce at least one single malt

Chalk sign hanging in Blackfish Spirits Distillery, by Carrie Gifford. *Photo credit: Becky Garrison.*

145

whiskey,[345] and the relaunch of the Washington Distillers Guild[346] speak to a burgeoning interest in Pacific Northwest craft spirits. With the rise of American single malt as a new spirits category and with Copperworks and Westland among the founding members of the ASMWC, coupled with Barnes's expertise in distilling and promoting single grain whiskeys, expect to see a surge in global demand for these spirits (especially whiskeys).[347]

Seems whiskey not only won the Pacific Northwest but the world as well. I'll drink to that.

Appendix

A TOUR OF WASHINGTON STATE DISTILLERIES

Seattle's Urban Distilleries

SODO/Downtown

Alphabet Vodka. https://www.drinkalphabet.com
Copperworks Distilling Company. https://copperworksdistilling.com
Glass Distillery. https://glassvodka.com
Letterpress Distilling. https://www.letterpressdistilling.com
OOLA Distillery. https://ooladistillery.com
2BAR Spirits. http://2barspirits.com
Westland Distillery. https://www.westlanddistillery.com

Queen Anne/Fremont

Big Gin Distillery. https://biggindistillery.com
Fast Penny Spirits. https://www.fastpennyspirits.com
Fremont Mischief Distillery. https://fremontmischief.com
Old Log Cabin. https://oldlogcabin.com
Skybound Spirits. https://www.skyboundspirits.com

GREATER SEATTLE (NORTH)

Bothell

Wildwood Spirits Co. https://wildwoodspiritsco.com

Duvall

Duvall Distillery. https://duvalldistillery.com

Edmonds

Scratch Distillery. https://scratchdistillery.com

Lynnwood

Temple Distilling Company. https://www.templedistilling.com

Maltby

J.P. Trodden Distilling. https://www.jptrodden.com

Snohomish

Skip Rock Distillers. https://www.skiprockdistillers.com
Wohlfert Craft Distilling. https://wohlfertcraftdistilling.com

Woodinville

BROVO Spirits. https://brovospirits.com
Copper Cat Distillery. https://www.coppercatdistillery.com
Northwest Spirits. https://northwestspirits.com
Pacific Distillery. https://pacificdistillery.com
Puget Sound Rum Company. http://www.pugetsoundrum.com
Woodinville Whiskey Co. http://www.woodinvillewhiskeyco.com

Northwest Washington

Arlington

Bad Dog Distillery. https://www.baddogdistillery.com

Bellingham

Chuckanut Bay Distillery. https://chuckanutbaydistillery.com

Edison

Terramar Brewing and Distilling. https://www.terramarcraft.com

Everett

Bluewater Organic Distilling. https://www.bluewaterdistilling.com
James Bay Distillers Ltd. https://www.jamesbaydistillers.com

Everson

Probably Shouldn't Distillery. https://www.probablyshouldntdistillery.com

Lynden

Bellewood Farmstead & Distillery. https://www.bellewooddistilling.com

Greater Seattle (South)

Auburn

Blackfish Spirits Distillery. https://www.blackfishdistillery.com

Edgewood

Nightside Distillery. https://nightsidedistillery.com

Enumclaw

Pursuit Distilling Co. https://www.pursuitdistilling.com

Gig Harbor

Heritage Distilling Company. http://heritagedistilling.com

Lakewood

Mastrogiannis Distillery & Winery. https://www.mastrogiannisdistillery.com

Port Orchard

Black Ring Spirits. https://www.blackringspirits.com

Tacoma

Old Soldier Distillery. https://oldsoldierdistillery.com

Tumwater

Olympia Distilling Co. & Shoebox Spirits. https://shoebox-spirits.business.site
Percival Creek https://thecraftdistrict.com/directory/percival-creek

University Place

Chambers Bay Distillery. https://chambersbaydistillery.com

SOUTHWEST WASHINGTON

Battleground

Battle Crest Distillary. https://www.battlecrestdistillary.com

Centralia

King Distillery. http://kingdistilleryllc.com/index.html

Rochester

Talking Cedar Brewery and Distillery. https://talkingcedar.com

Stevenson

Skunk Brothers Spirits. http://skunkbrothersspirits.com

Tenino

Sandstone Distillery. https://www.sandstonedistillery.com

Vancouver

Quartz Mountain Distillers. https://quartzmountaindistillers.com

THE ISLANDS

Bainbridge Island

Bainbridge Organic Distillers. http://www.bainbridgedistillers.com
Highside Distilling. https://www.highsidedistilling.com

Long Beach Peninsula

Adrift Distillers. https://adriftdistillers.com

San Juan Islands/Anacortes

Orcas Island Distillery https://orcasislanddistillery.com/
San Juan Island Distillery. https://www.sanjuanislanddistillery.com
Wheelhouse Distillery. https://www.yelp.com/biz/wheelhouse-distillery-anacortes

Whidbey Island

Cultus Bay Distillery. https://cultusbaydistillery.com
Whidbey Island Distillery. https://www.whidbeydistillery.com

OLYMPIC PENINSULA

Aberdeen

Westport Winery Garden Resort and Ocean's Daughters Distillery. https://
www.westportwinery.com

Hoodsport

Hardware Distillery Co. https://www.thehardwaredistillery.com

Port Angeles

Caudill Bros. Distillery. https://caudillbrosdistillery.com
Port Angeles Distilling Company. http://www.portangelesdistilling.com

Port Townsend

Admiralty Distillers. http://admiraltydistillers.com

CENTRAL AND EASTERN WASHINGTON

Ellensburg

Elk Heights Distillery. http://www.elkheightsdistillery.com

Leavenworth

Blue Spirits Distilling. https://www.bluespiritsdistilling.com

Loon Lake

2 Loons Distillery. https://2loonsdistillery.com

Prosser

Monson Ranch Distillers. https://monsonranchdistillers.com

Richland

Solar Spirits. https://solarspirits.com

Spokane

Browne Family Spirits. https://brownefamilyvineyards.com/spirits
Dry Fly Distilling. https://dryflydistilling.com

Sultan

Curtson Distillery. https://www.curtson.com

Walla Walla

Cedar Rain Spirits. https://www.cedarrainspirits.com
DW Distilling. http://www.dwdistilling.net
Shot in the Dark Craft Distillery. https://hetterleys.com
2nd Street Distilling Company. https://2ndstreetdistillingco.com

West Richland

Black Heron. https://drinkblackheron.com

Yakima

Distillarium. https://thedistillarium.com
Swede Hill Distilling. https://swedehilldistilling.com
Wilridge Winery & Distillery. https://www.wilridgewinery.com

Zillah

Vitis Spirits. https://www.vitisspirits.com

For the most up-to-date listing of Washington State distilleries in current operation, log on to the Washington Distillery Trail website at https://www.washingtondistillerytrail.com.

NOTES

Preface

1. Garrison, *Little Book of Virtues*, 72–73.
2. See Garrison, "Gaslighting for God."

Introduction

3. Forsyth, *Short History of Drunkenness*, 183.
4. Rorabaugh, *Alcoholic Republic*, 69.
5. Skagit County Historical Society, email correspondence.
6. Mitenbuler, *Bourbon Empire*, 19.
7. E. Burns, *Spirits of America*, 8.
8. Bashone, email correspondence, August 24, 2023.
9. Forsyth, *Short History of Drunkenness*, 183.
10. Rorabaugh, *Alcoholic Republic*, 112–13.
11. Forsyth, *Short History of Drunkenness*, 184.
12. See Marcy, *Prairie and Overland Traveller*.
13. While Old Crow is now viewed as cheap rotgut, in Mark Twain's time this spirit was revered as the gold standard in whiskey.
14. Twain, *Life on the Mississippi*, 586–87.
15. Statista.com, "Operating Craft Distilleries."
16. Fisher, "States That Drink."
17. National Park Service, "Oregon Territory."
18. Mole, *Scoundrels and Saloons*, 8–9.

Chapter 1

19. Huckelbridge, *Bourbon*, 152.
20. Cheever, *Drinking in America*, 130–31.
21. Mob Museum, "Medicine and Poison."
22. Huckelbridge, *Bourbon*, 152–55.
23. Schrad, *Smashing the Liquor Machine*, 262.
24. Walker, "Liquor Laws."
25. WA Wine, "History."
26. Liang, "Fort Vancouver Treasures."
27. The history of alcohol and distilling at Fort Vancouver can be found at the Fort Vancouver National Historic Site and in Stursa, *Distilled in Oregon*, 24–25.
28. Mole, *Scoundrels and Saloons*, 17.
29. Stursa, *Distilled in Oregon*, 30-31.
30. Mole, *Scoundrels and Saloons*, 17–18, 77.
31. Forsyth, *Short History of Drunkenness*, 185.
32. Mole, *Scoundrels and Saloons*, 18.
33. Irvine, *Wine Project*, 49, 51.
34. Forsyth, *Short History of Drunkenness*, 185.
35. Mole, *Scoundrels and Saloons*, 73.
36. Schwantes, *Pacific Northwest*, 301.
37. National Park Service, "Klondike Gold Rush."
38. Mole, *Scoundrels and Saloons*, 73, 79, 63, 109, 112.
39. English, *Doctors and Distillers*, 209–10.
40. *Mason County Journal*, November 9, 1894.
41. Troy, "Origin of Word 'Hooch.'"
42. Joyce, *Moonshine*, 14.
43. *Seattle Post-Intelligencer*, November 15, 1891; September 2, 1884.
44. *Spokesman-Review*, July 26, 1927.
45. *Walla Walla Statesman*, December 2, 1864; March 31, 1865; December 6, 1867.
46. Washington State Archives, "Collection of Bankruptcy Papers."
47. *Puget Sound Weekly Argus*, July 27, 1877.
48. *Washington Standard*, September 26, 1890.
49. *Seattle Post-Intelligencer*, November 17, 1890.
50. *Spokane Review*, March 27, 1893.
51. *Washington Standard*, November 23, 1894.
52. *Pullman Herald*, March 23, 1894; July 27, 1894.
53. *Seattle Post-Intelligencer*, February 14, 1894; March 29, 1894; January 6, 1895; July 2, 1897.
54. *Yakima Herald*, April 5, 1894.
55. *Dawn*, July 6, 1895.
56. *Seattle Post-Intelligencer*, February 1, 1891.
57. *Spokane Falls Review*, February 28, 1889.
58. *Pullman Herald*, November 17, 1888; September 29, 1900.

59. *Adams County News*, May 9, 1900.
60. *Seattle Post-Intelligencer*, December 23, 1890.
61. pre-pro.com Distillery Database, "Warehouse Records."
62. *Seattle Star*, September 28, 1905; March 17, 1906.
63. *Spokane Press*, August 26, 1907.
64. *Yakima Herald*, August 28, 1907.
65. pre-pro.com Distillery Database, "City Directory Listings Database."
66. Barnes, email correspondence.
67. *1914 Yakima County*, 354.
68. Joyce, *Moonshine*, 43.
69. Okrent, *Last Call*, 30.
70. *Washington Standard*, March 24, 1899.
71. *Skagit River Journal*, "Otto Peterson."
72. Joyce, *Moonshine*, 47, 55.
73. English, *Doctors and Distillers*, 212.
74. Mob Museum, "Medicine and Poison."

Chapter 2

75. Forsyth, *Short History of Drunkenness*, 214.
76. Clark, *Dry Years*, 61.
77. Perry, email correspondence.
78. E. Burns, *Spirits of America*, 147.
79. Soden, "Woman's Christian Temperance Union," 198.
80. Collins, *Good Time Girls*, 20–21.
81. Mole, *Scoundrels and Saloons*, 83.
82. Cleveland, "Here Are 10 Things."
83. Snopes.com, "Shot of Whiskey."
84. Filson Journal, "Origin of 'Skid Row.'"
85. Broderick, *Seattle's Old Saloons*.
86. Mole, *Scoundrels and Saloons*, 83.
87. Soden, "Woman's Christian Temperance Union," 198.
88. Pfeiffer-Hoyt, phone interview.
89. Cheever, *Drinking in America*, 3.
90. Wood, "15 Fun Phrases."
91. Schrad, *Smashing the Liquor Machine*, 457, 536.
92. Rorabaugh, *Prohibition*, 37.
93. Schrad, *Smashing the Liquor Machine*, 457.
94. Troy, "There's No Such Thing."
95. Schrad, *Smashing the Liquor Machine*, 457.
96. Blecha, "Durkin, James."
97. Broderick, *Seattle's Old Saloons*.
98. Weber/Roochvarg, "Evangelist Billy Sunday."
99. Soden, "Matthews, Reverend Mark."

100. Clark, *Dry Years*, 64.
101. Coleman, *Peerless Collection*, 5.
102. Schrad, *Smashing the Liquor Machine*, 457.
103. Andrews, "Woman's Christian Temperance Union."
104. Clark, *Dry Years*, 35.
105. Soden, "Woman's Christian Temperance Union," 200–01.
106. E. Burns, *Spirits of America*, 151.
107. Schrad, *Smashing the Liquor Machine*, 465.
108. Clark, *Dry Years*, 73, 67.
109. WashingtonVotes.org, "2008 House Bill 2959."
110. Andrews, "Woman's Christian Temperance Union."
111. Constitution Annotated, "Nineteenth Amendment."
112. Becker, "Prohibition in Washington State."
113. Mole, *Scoundrels and Saloons*, 112.
114. MOHAI, "City Hall Jail.'"
115. LeSourd, "Blue Laws—Washington State."
116. Weber/Roochvarg, "Evangelist Billy Sunday."
117. Mole, *Scoundrels and Saloons*, 97, 109–10.
118. Clark, *Dry Years*, 106.
119. Okrent, *Last Call*, 83–84, 103.
120. Minnick, *Bourbon*, 74, 80.
121. Mole, *Scoundrels and Saloons*, 127.
122. Blecha and Holden, *Lost Roadhouses of Seattle*, 16.
123. English, *Doctors and Distillers*, 220.
124. Seattle Municipal Archives, "Prohibition in Seattle."
125. Blecha and Holden, *Lost Roadhouses of Seattle*, 16.
126. Holden, "Prohibition."
127. Minnick, *Bourbon*, 81, 87.
128. Becker, "Prohibition in Washington State."
129. FBI, "A Byte Out of History."
130. *Seattle Daily Times*, September 26, 1919.

Chapter 3

131. Seattle Municipal Archives, "Prohibition in Seattle."
132. *Merriam-Webster*, "8 Prohibition-Era Words."
133. Minnick, *Bourbon*, 92, 102, 100.
134. Okrent, *Last Call*, 193–94.
135. Minnick, *Bourbon*, 92.
136. Owens et al., *Art of Distilling*, 18.
137. Klein, "America's Iconic Brewers."
138. Rorabaugh, *Prohibition*, 67.
139. Holden, *Seattle Prohibition*, 60.
140. Ibid., 64; Holden, "Prohibition."

141. Britannica, "Bootlegging."
142. Holden, "Prohibition."
143. ABC Bookworld, "Rumrunner."
144. Holden, *Seattle Prohibition*, 102–3; Holden, "Prohibition."
145. Anderson, "Smugglers, Rumrunners and Bootleggers."
146. Becker, "Prohibition in Washington State."
147. Smith Tower, "Characters Exhibit Experience."
148. Holden, *Seattle Prohibition*, 49, 52; Holden, "Prohibition."
149. Billock, "Moonshine Bootlegging."
150. Metcalfe, *Whispering Wires*, 196.
151. Holden, *Seattle Prohibition*, 79.
152. K. Burns, "Prohibition: Whispering Wires."
153. Editors of Publications International, "Golden Age of Flight."
154. Freeman, "Abandoned & Little-Known."
155. *Bellingham Herald*, July 14, 1927; October 20, 1928; February 7, 1929; May 8, 1929; May 24, 1929; June 15, 1929; June 17, 1929.
156. *Daily Olympian*, April 17, 1929.
157. *Chilliwack Progress*, March 17, 1932.
158. Troth, email interview.
159. *Spokesman-Review*, September 23, 2023.
160. *Everett Daily Herald*, June 19, 1925.
161. Private collection of Ernest Troth.
162. English, *Doctors and Distillers*, 253–54.
163. E. Burns, *Spirits of America*, 218, 220, 224.
164. Okrent, *Last Call*, 210–11.
165. Graham, "What Is a Cocktail?"
166. Wood, "15 Fun Phrases."
167. Holden, *Seattle Prohibition*, 52, 45–46, 84, 102.
168. *Merriam-Webster*, "Scofflaw."
169. Anderson, "Smugglers, Rumrunners and Bootleggers."
170. Arskey, "Booze Routes to Spokane."
171. *Merriam-Webster*, "8 Prohibition-Era Words."
172. *Seattle Star*, May 28, 1925.
173. *Spokesman-Review*, December 14, 1929.
174. Haulman, *Vashon Island*, 90, 110–11.
175. Black Diamond Historical Society, "Mary Draghi."
176. *Seattle Star*, March 8, 1924.
177. Varney, *Ghost Towns*, 46.
178. Pfeiffer-Hoyt, phone interview.
179. Rorabaugh, "Washington State Liquor Control Board, 1934," 161.
180. Becker, "Prohibition in Washington State."
181. Clark, *Dry Years*, 241.
182. Klein, "Night Prohibition Ended."
183. *Spokesman-Review*, November 11, 1933.

Chapter 4

184. Rorabaugh, "Washington State Liquor Control Board, 1934," 161.
185. NABCA, "Three-Tier System."
186. *Seattle Times*, "Liquor Control Board."
187. Becker, "Governor Clarence Martin."
188. Clark, *Dry Years*, 242–43.
189. Becker, "Governor Clarence Martin."
190. Waugh, "Guide to the Records."
191. Forsyth, *Short History of Drunkenness*, 223.
192. Becker, "Governor Clarence Martin."
193. Irvine, *Wine Project*, 144.
194. Gann, "Sound Spirits Celebrates."
195. *Veterans' Review*, November 15, 1936.
196. *Northwest Enterprise*, "Wash. Industry Reveals Progress."
197. Gann, "Sound Spirits Celebrates."
198. Rorabaugh, "Washington State Liquor Control Board," 164.
199. Minnick, *Bourbon*, 191.
200. Cummings, "Backstage Olympia."
201. Waugh, "Washington State Liquor Control Board."
202. Minnick, *Bourbon*, 157.
203. Cummings, "Backstage Olympia."
204. Clark, *Dry Years*, 247, 245.
205. Blecha and Holden, *Lost Roadhouses of Seattle*, 19.
206. Rorabaugh, "Washington State Liquor Control Board," 165.
207. Waugh, "Washington State Liquor Control Board."
208. Clark, *Dry Years*, 248.
209. Waugh, "Washington State Liquor Control Board"
210. LeSourd, "Blue Laws—Washington State."
211. Clark, *Dry Years*, 270.
212. Waugh, "Washington State Liquor Control Board."
213. Jenkins, "Alcohol Impact."
214. Dietrich, "Dry Fly Distilling."
215. Dry Fly Distilling website.
216. WashingtonVotes.org, "2008 House Bill 2959."
217. Poffenroth, email interview.
218. LCB, "Distillery FAQ."
219. LCB, "Craft Distilleries License."
220. Washington Secretary of State, "Initiative Measure No. 1183."
221. Becker, "Prohibition in Washington State."
222. Wilkinson, "Liquor Won't Be Sold."
223. Fritts, "How Stiff?"
224. Beveridge, phone interview.
225. LCB, "Farmers Market Authorization/Endorsement."

226. LCB, "Distillery FAQ."
227. LCB, "Added Activities."
228. LCB, "Retail Liquor Licenses"; Washington State Legislature, "SB 5448-2023-24.
229. Congress.gov, "H.R.337."
230. TTB, "Home Distilling."
231. BoozeMakers.com, "U.S. Home Distilling Laws."
232. Washington State Legislature, "RCW 66.44.140."
233. TTB, "Distilled Spirits Labeling."
234. Krogstad, email correspondence.

Chapter 5

235. Garrison, "American Single Malts in the Northwest."
236. Frost, "Terroir," 722–23.
237. Garrison, "Rise of American Single Malt Whiskey."
238. Stranahan's website.
239. Hofmann, in-person interview.
240. Pike Brewing Company website.
241. Salmon-Safe website.
242. ADI, "Copperworks Distilling Company."
243. Garrison, "Raising"; Parker, in-person interview.
244. ASMWC website.
245. Risen, "American Single Malt."
246. ADI, "American Single Malt."

Chapter 6

247. *Spokesman-Review*, "How Many Craft Distilleries?"
248. ADI, "U.S. Craft Distilleries."
249. Kallas-Lewis, email interview.
250. Alphabet Vodka website.
251. Kaiser, in-person interview.
252. Glass Distillery website.
253. Tognetti, phone interview.
254. Central Saloon, "History."
255. Smith Tower, "Characters Exhibit Experience."
256. Myers, in-person interview.
257. Stock, "Alcohol Brands."
258. Gann, "Sound Spirits Celebrates."
259. Sound Spirits, "sound.spirits." (Instagram).
260. Women's Cocktail Collective website.
261. Hunt, phone interview.

262. Old Log Cabin website.
263. Skybound Spirits website.
264. Silva, phone interview.
265. Liedholm, email interview.
266. Edmonds Localvore website.
267. Karrick, in-person GINiology™ workshop and email interview.
268. Temple, phone interview and in-person visit.
269. Nesheim, email interview.
270. Wohlfert, phone interview.
271. Hembree, phone interview.
272. Woodinville Whiskey Company website.
273. LVMH, "Moët Hennessy Acquires."
274. Voelsgen, email correspondence.
275. Copper Cat Distillery website.
276. Kelly, email interview.
277. Warren, email interview.
278. TTB, "Term Absinthe."
279. Artisan Hill website.
280. Bernhard, email interview.
281. Duvall Distillery, email correspondence.
282. Lundin, email interview.
283. Troth, email interview.
284. Barker, email interview.
285. Lynette, email interview.
286. LaBree, email interview; Bellinghistory with the Good Time Girls' Sin & Gin Tours.
287. Bellewood Farmstead & Distillery website.
288. McGlothern, email interview.
289. Butenschoen, phone interview.
290. Gifford, phone interview and in-person visit.
291. Greene, email interview.
292. Agnew, phone interview; Crux Fermentation Project, "Introducing: Our First Whiskey!"
293. Old Soldier Distillery website.
294. Mastrogiannis, email interview.
295. Smiley, email interview.
296. Martin, email interview.
297. Chambers Bay Distillery website.
298. Sagawa, email correspondence.
299. Givens, email interview.
300. Bourdon, phone interview.
301. DeMauro, email interview.
302. King Distillery website.
303. Schefers, email interview.

304. Quartz Mountain Distillers website.
305. Skunk Brothers Spirits website.
306. Marano, "Bainbridge Organic Distillers."
307. Lindenmuth, "Bainbridge YAMA."
308. Scarsella, "Bainbridge Organic Distillers."
309. Barnes, in-person visit.
310. Glenn, in-person visit and email interview.
311. Wheelhouse Distillery website.
312. Orcas Island Distillery website.
313. Pingree, email interview.
314. Huffman, email interview.
315. Parks, email interview.
316. Davidson, email interview.
317. Degerman, "Westport Winery Garden Resort."
318. Roberts, email interview.
319. Churcher, email interview.
320. Caudill, email interview.
321. Soule, email interview.
322. Morris, phone interview.
323. Curtson Distillery website.
324. Blue Spirits Distilling website.
325. Brick Saloon website.
326. Meyers, "It Happened Here."
327. Elk Heights Distillery website.
328. Beveridge, phone interview.
329. Rasmussen, email interview.
330. Swede Hill Distilling website.
331. Leone, email correspondence.
332. Bluebird Inn website.
333. Denci, email interview.
334. Williams, email correspondence.
335. Watt, phone interview.
336. Schiro, email interview.
337. DW Distilling, email correspondence.
338. Cedar Rain Spirits website.
339. Hetterley, email correspondence.
340. Fogarty, email interview.
341. Schwartz, email interview.

Chapter 7

342. Poffenroth, email interview.
343. Cooper, "Last Year."
344. Barnes, in-person visit.

345. Northwest Whiskey Trail website.
346. Washington Distillers Guild.
347. ASMWC website.

BIBLIOGRAPHY

ABC Bookworld. "Rumrunner: The Life and Times of Johnny Schnarr." December 13, 2003. https://abcbookworld.com/article/article-13119.

Agnew, Sam. Phone interview, July 28, 2023.

Alcohol and Tobacco Tax and Trade Bureau (TTB). "Distilled Spirits Labeling." https://www.ttb.gov/distilled-spirits/labeling.

———. "Home Distilling." https://www.ttb.gov/distilled-spirits/penalties-for-illegal-distilling.

———. "Use of the Term Absinthe for Distilled Spirits." https://www.ttb.gov/images/industry_circulars/archives/2007/07-05.html.

Alphabet Vodka. https://www.drinkalphabet.com.

American Distilling Institute (ADI). "American Single Malt." https://distilling.com/spirit/american-single-malt.

———. "Copperworks Distilling Company." https://web.distilling.com/Distillery/Copperworks-Distilling-Co-519.

———. "U.S. Craft Distilleries by State." July 15, 2022. https://distilling.com/resources/data.

American Single Malt Whiskey Commission (ASMWC). https://www.americansinglemaltwhiskey.org.

Anderson, Peter. "Smugglers, Rumrunners and Bootleggers." Mukilteo Historical Society. May 9, 2020. https://mukilteohistorical.org/2020/05/08/muk-revisited-prohibition.

Andrews, Mildred. "Woman's Christian Temperance Union Western Washington." HistoryLink.org. December 2, 1998. https://historylink.org/File/407.

Arskey, Laura. "Prohibition: Booze Routes to Spokane." March 9, 2011. HistoryLink.org. https://www.historylink.org/File/9702.

Artisan Hill. https://www.artisanhill.com.

Barker, Chris. Email interview, May 8, 2023.

Barnes, Keith. In-person visit, May 10, 2023, and email correspondence, July 22, 2023.

Bashone, Steve. Email correspondence, August 24, 2023. https://www.mountvernon.org/the-estate-gardens/distillery.

Becker, Paula. "Governor Clarence Martin Signs the Steele Act Establishing the Washington State Liquor Control Board on January 23, 1934." HistoryLink.org, January 17, 2011. https://www.historylink.org/File/9692.

———. "Prohibition in Washington State." HistoryLink.org, November 20, 2010. https://www.historylink.org/File/9630.

Bellewood Farmstead & Distillery. https://www.bellewooddistilling.com.

Bernhard, Marc. Email interview, May 12, 2023.

Beveridge, Paul. Phone interview, November 5, 2022.

Billock, Jennifer. "How Moonshine Bootlegging Gave Rise to NASCAR: Rotgut and Firewater Are the Founding Fathers of Our Nation's Racing Pastime." *Smithsonian Magazine*, February 10, 2017. https://www.smithsonianmag.com/travel/how-moonshine-bootlegging-gave-rise-nascar-180962014.

Black Diamond Historical Society. "Mary Draghi, Queen of the Foothill Bootleggers." Information courtesy of Louis Draghi.

Blecha, Peter. "Durkin, James (1859–1934)." HistoryLink.org, June 21, 2009. https://www.historylink.org/File/9018.

Blecha, Peter, and Brad Holden. *Lost Roadhouses of Seattle*. Charleston, SC: The History Press, 2022.

Bluebird Inn. http://www.bickleton.org/bluebird-inn.

Blue Spirits Distilling. https://www.bluespiritsdistilling.com.

BoozeMakers.com. "U.S. Home Distilling Laws by State." https://boozemakers.com/home-distilling-laws-by-state.

Bourdon, John. Phone interview, April 5, 2023.

Brick Saloon. https://www.bricksaloon.com.

Britannica. "Bootlegging." https://www.britannica.com/topic/bootlegging.

Broderick, Henry. *Seattle's Old Saloons*. Seattle: Dogwood Press, 1966.

Burns, Eric. *The Spirits of America: A Social History of Alcohol*. Philadelphia: Temple University Press, 2004.

Burns, Ken. "Prohibition: Whispering Wires." *PBS*, October 2, 2011. https://www.pbs.org/video/prohibition-whispering-wires-whispering-wires.

Butenschoen, Mariah. Phone interview, April 3, 2023.

Caudill, Mike. Email interview, February 28, 2023.

Cedar Rain Spirits. https://www.cedarrainspirits.com.

Central Saloon. "History." https://www.centralsaloon.com/history.

Chambers Bay Distillery. https://chambersbaydistillery.com.

Cheever, Susan. *Drinking in America*. New York: Twelve, 2015.

Churcher, Cynthia. Email interview, June 30, 2023.

Clark, Norman H. *The Dry Years: Prohibition and Social Change in Washington*. 2nd revised ed. Seattle: University of Washington Press, 1988.

Cleveland, Nikki. "Here Are 10 Things They Don't Teach You About Washington in School." Only in Your State, March 9, 2016. https://www.onlyinyourstate.com/washington/dont-teach-in-wa.

Coleman, Emmet G., ed. *A Peerless Collection of Temperance Songs and Hymns for Christian Women's Temperance Union, Loyal Temperance Legion, Prohibitionists, Temperance Praise Meetings, Medal Contests, etc.* New York: American Heritage Press, 1971. First published 1907. Page references are to the 1971 edition.

Collins, Jan McKell. *Good Time Girls of the Pacific Northwest: A Red-Light History of Washington, Oregon, and Alaska.* Lanham, MD: TwoDot, 2020.

Congress.gov. "H.R.337." https://www.congress.gov/bill/95th-congress/house-bill/1337.

Constitution Annotated. "Constitution of the United States: Nineteenth Amendment." https://constitution.congress.gov/constitution/amendment-19.

Cooper, Chasity. "Last Year, the Drinks Industry Made a Commitment to Diversity. Here's What Has Changed." Seven-Fifty Daily, September 27, 2021. https://daily.sevenfifty.com/last-year-the-drinks-industry-made-a-commitment-to-diversity-heres-what-has-changed/.

Copper Cat Distillery. https://www.coppercatdistillery.com.

Crux Fermentation Project. "Introducing: Our First Whiskey!" https://www.cruxfermentation.com/2022/02/15/straight-bourbon-whiskey.

Cummings, Robert. "Backstage Olympia." *Bellingham Herald*, December 21, 1967.

Curtson Distillery. https://www.curtson.com.

Davidson, Sara Ann. Email interview, February 7, 2023.

Degerman, Eric. "2022 Washington Winery of the Year: Westport Winery Garden Resort." *Great Northwest Wine*, April 12, 2022. https://greatnorthwestwine.com/2022/04/12/2022-washington-winery-of-the-year-westport-winery-garden-resort.

DeMauro, Francesca (KCSA Strategic Communications). Email interview, May 31, 2023.

Denci, Patricia (Double Forte). Email interview, August 3, 2023.

Dietrich, Heidi. "Talking with Don Poffenroth and Kent Fleischmann, Owners of Dry Fly Distilling." *Puget Sound Business Journal*, December 9, 2007. https://www.bizjournals.com/seattle/stories/2007/12/10/story14.html.

Dry Fly Distilling. "Our Story." https://dryflydistilling.com/pages/our-story.

Duvall Distillery. https://duvalldistillery.com.

DW Distilling. Email correspondence, August 26, 2023. http://dwbrandy.com.

Editors of Publications International Ltd. "The Heart of the Golden Age of Flight." HowStuffWorks. https://science.howstuffworks.com/transport/flight/classic/golden-age-of-flight.htm.

Edmonds Localvore. https://www.edmondslocalvore.com.

Elk Heights Distillery. http://www.elkheightsdistillery.com.

English, Camper. *Doctors and Distillers.* New York: Penguin Random House, 2022.

Federal Bureau of Investigation. "A Byte Out of History: 'Machine Gun' Kelly and the Legend of the G-Men." September 26, 2003. https://archives.fbi.gov/archives/news/stories/2003/september/kelly092603.

Filson Journal. "Yesler Way: This History & Origin of 'Skid Row.'" https://www.filson.com/blog/field-notes/yesler-way-the-true-story-behind-skid-row.

Fisher, Andrew. "The States That Drink the Most Alcohol in America (2022)." Alcohol Delivered, April 10, 2023. https://alcoholdelivered.com.au/blog/map-states-drink-alcohol-america.

Fogarty, Erin. (Precept Wine). Email interview, August 10, 2023.

Forsyth, Mark. *A Short History of Drunkenness: How, Why, Where and When Humankind Has Gotten Merry from the Stone Age to the Present*. New York: Crown Publishing, 2018.

Fort Vancouver National Historic Site. https://www.nps.gov/fova/index.htm.

Freeman, Paul. "Abandoned & Little-Known Airfields, Washington: Seattle Area." Revised August 15, 2023. http://www.airfields-freeman.com/WA/Airfields_WA_Seattle.htm#ebey.

Fritts, Janelle. "How Stiff Are Distilled Spirits Taxes in Your State?" Tax Foundation, June 16, 2021. https://taxfoundation.org/data/all/state/state-distilled-spirits-taxes-2021.

Frost, Doug. "Terroir." In *The Oxford Companion to Spirits and Cocktails*, edited by David Wondrich and Noah Rothbaum. New York: Oxford University Press, 2022.

Gann, Brian. "Sound Spirits Celebrates Its Grand Opening and Likely Becomes the First Legal Distillery in Seattle Since the 1930s on September 18, 2010." HistoryLink.org, January 25, 2011. https://www.historylink.org/File/9697.

Garrison, Becky. "Gaslighting for God, Parts 1–8." Wittenburg Door (Substack), March 2–April 20, 2022. https://substack.com/@wittenburgdoor.

———. "Raising Capitol for Spirits Through Crowdfunding." *Beverage Master*, December 2, 2020. https://beverage-master.com/2020/12/raising-capital-for-craft-spirits-through-crowdfunding.

———. "The Rise of American Single Malts in the Northwest." *SIP*, May 30, 2023. https://sipmagazine.com/the-rise-of-american-single-malts-in-the-northwest.

———. "The Rise of American Single Malt Whiskey." *Beverage Master*, October 10, 2019. https://beverage-master.com/2019/10/the-rise-of-american-single-malt-whiskey.

———. *Roger Williams's Little Book of Virtues*. Eugene, OR: Wipf & Stock, 2020.

Gifford, Mike. Phone interview, March 1, 2023, and in-person visit, May 11, 2023.

Givens, Lesa. Email interview, August 2, 2023.

Glass Distillery. https://glassvodka.com.

Glenn, Matt. In-person visit, May 10, 2023, and email interview, May 5, 2023.

Graham, Colleen. "What Is a Cocktail?" Spruce Eats, September 19, 2022. https://www.thespruceeats.com/what-is-a-cocktail-760163.

Greene, Tom. Email interview, February 2, 2023.

Harden, Blaine. *Murder at the Mission: A Frontier Killing, Its Legacy of Lies, and the Taking of the American West*. New York: Viking Press, 2021.

Haulman, Bruce. *A Brief History of Vashon Island*. Charleston, SC: The History Press, 2015.

Hembree, Ryan. Phone interview, February 28, 2023.

Hetterley, Betsy. Email correspondence, October 23, 2024

Hofmann, Matt. In-person interview, March 24, 2023.

Holden, Brad. "Prohibition in the Puget Sound Region (1916–1933)." HistoryLink.org, November 18, 2019. https://www.historylink.org/File/20904.

———. *Seattle Prohibition: Bootleggers, Rumrunners & Graft in the Queen City.* Charleston, SC: The History Press, 2019.

Huckelbridge, Dane. *Bourbon: A History of the American Spirit.* New York: William Morrow, 2014.

Huffman, Mike. Email interview, April 7, 2023.

Hunt, Jamie. Phone interview, May 11, 2023.

Irvine, Ronald. *The Wine Project: Washington State's Winemaking History.* Vashon, WA: Sketch Publications, 1977.

Jenkins, Laura. "Alcohol Impact Area Information and Updates—Neighborhoods." Seattle.gov, November 2, 2022. https://www.seattle.gov/neighborhoods/programs-and-services/alcohol-impact-area-information-and-updates.

Joyce, Jamie. *Moonshine: A Cultural History of America's Infamous Liquor.* Minneapolis: Zenith Press, 2014.

Kaiser, Nathan. In-person interview, March 24, 2023.

Kallas-Lewis, Kirby. Email interview, April 7, 2023.

Karrick, Kim. In-person GINiology™ workshop, April 2, 2023, and email interview, April 11, 2023.

Kelly, Tom. Email interview, May 9, 2023.

Kershner, Jim, "100 Years Ago in Spokane: A Chronicle Exposé Shed Light on the Seamy Industry of Aerial Bootlegging." *Spokesman-Review,* September 23, 2023. https://www.spokesman.com/stories/2023/sep/20/100-years-ago-in-spokane-a-chronicle-expose-shed-l.

King Distillery. http://kingdistilleryllc.com/index.html.

Klein, Christopher. "How America's Iconic Brewers Survived Prohibition." History.com, January 29, 2019. https://www.history.com/news/brewers-under-prohibition-miller-coors-busch-yuengling-pabst.

———. "The Night Prohibition Ended." History.com, December 5, 2013. https://www.history.com/news/the-night-prohibition-ended.

Krogstad, Christian. Email correspondence, May 11, 2023.

LaBree, Kolby. Email interview, May 9, 2023; Bellinghistory with the Good Time Girls' Sin & Gin Tours, https://bellinghistory.com/sin-and-gin-tours.

LaCapria, Kim, and David Emery. "Did the Phrase 'A Shot of Whiskey' Originate in the Old West?" Snopes.com, October 14, 2017. https://www.snopes.com/fact-check/shot-whiskey-origin.

Leone, Sal. Email correspondence, July 25, 2023.

LeSourd, Peter. "Blue Laws—Washington State." HistoryLink.org, June 20, 2009. https://www.historylink.org/File/9057.

Liang, Michael. "Fort Vancouver Treasures." Ranger Mike Designs: Inspiration for the National Park Service, January 21, 2010. https://rangermikedesigns.wordpress.com/2010/01/21/fort-vancouver-treasures.

Liedholm, Erik. Email interview, February 24, 2023.

Lindenmuth, Jeffrey. "2016 Craft Whiskey of the Year: Bainbridge YAMA." *Whiskey Advocate*, December 9, 2016. https://whiskyadvocate.com/2016-craft-whiskey-of-the-year.

Lundin, John. Email interview, May 19, 2023.

Lynette, Ethan. Email interview, March 15, 2023.

Marano, Luciano. "Bainbridge Organic Distillers Uncorks New Yama-inspired Whiskey." *Bainbridge Island Review*, April 8, 2016. https://www.bainbridgereview.com/news/bainbridge-organic-distillers-uncorks-new-yama-inspired-whiskey.

Marcy, R.B. *The Prairie and Overland Traveller, A Companion for Emigrants, Traders, Travellers, Hunters and Soldiers Traversing Great Plains and Prairies.* London: Sampson Low, Son, 1860.

Martin, Tom. Email interview, April 16, 2023.

Mastrogiannis, Ilias. Email interview, March 5, 2023.

McGlothern, Shelly. Email interview, April 4, 2023.

Merriam-Webster. "8 Prohibition-Era Words." https://www.merriam-webster.com/wordplay/Prohibition-era-words.

———. "Scofflaw." https://www.merriam-webster.com/dictionary/scofflaw.

Metcalfe, Philip. *Whispering Wires: The Tragic Tale of an American Bootlegger.* Portland, OR: Inkwater Press, 2021.

Meyers, Donald W. "It Happened Here: The Brick Is one of Washington's Oldest Saloons." *Yakima Herald-Republic*, June 3, 2019. https://www.yakimaherald.com/news/local/happened/it-happened-here-the-brick-is-one-of-washingtons-oldest-saloons/article_6119ba75-96f2-52a5-be4e-9709d5331c50.html.

Minnick, Fred. *Bourbon: The Rise, Fall and Rebirth of an American Whiskey.* Beverly, MA: Voyageur Press, 2016.

Mitenbuler, Reid. *Bourbon Empire: The Past and Present of America's Whiskey.* New York: Penguin Random House, 2015.

The Mob Museum. "Alcohol as Medicine and Poison." Prohibition: An Interactive History. https://prohibition.themobmuseum.org/the-history/the-prohibition-underworld/alcohol-as-medicine-and-poison.

Moët Hennessy Louis Vuitton (LVMH). "Moët Hennessy Acquires Washington's Woodinville Whiskey Company," July 13, 2017. https://www.lvmh.com/news-documents/press-releases/moet-hennessy-acquires-washingtons-woodinville-whiskey-company.

Mole, Rich. *Scoundrels and Saloons: Whisky Wars of the Pacific Northwest 1840–1917.* Toronto: Heritage House, 2012.

Morris, Jan. Phone interview, April 5, 2023.

Museum of History & Industry (MOHAI). "City Hall 'Jail,' and Effigies, Kirkland, Washington, 1907." https://digitalcollections.lib.washington.edu/digital/collection/imlsmohai/id/7077.

Myers, Alex. In-person interview, March 27, 2023.

National Alcohol Beverage Control Association (NABCA). "The Three-Tier System: A Modern View." https://www.nabca.org/three-tier-system-modern-view-0.

National Park Service. "Formation of the Oregon Territory." Last updated August 6, 2022. https://www.nps.gov/places/formation-of-the-oregon-territory.htm.

———. "Klondike Gold Rush-Seattle Unit." https://www.nps.gov/klse/index.htm.

Nesheim, Mark. Email interview, April 4, 2023.

The 1914 Yakima County & North Yakima Buyers Guide. Seattle: R.L. Polk, 1914.

Northwest Enterprise. "Wash. Industry Reveals Progress." January 14, 1938.

Northwest Whiskey Trail. https://northwestwhiskeytrail.com.

Okrent, Daniel. *Last Call: The Rise and Fall of Prohibition.* New York: Scribner, 2011.

Old Log Cabin. https://oldlogcabin.com.

Old Soldier Distillery. https://oldsoldierdistillery.com.

Orcas Island Distillery. https://orcasislanddistillery.com.

Owens, Bill, et al. *The Art of Distilling, Revised and Expanded: An Enthusiast's Guide to the Artisan Distilling of Whiskey, Vodka, Gin and other Potent Potables.* Beverly, MA: Quarry Books, 2019.

Parker, Jason. In-person interview, March 27, 2023.

Parks, Kathy. Email interview, May 5, 2023.

Perry, Madilane. Email correspondence, March 27, 2023, and June 5, 2023.

Pfeiffer-Hoyt, Russ. Phone interview, April 25, 2023.

Pike Brewing Company. http://www.pikebrewing.com.

Pingree, Suzy. Email interview, March 9, 2023.

Poffenroth, Don. Email interview, February 9, 2023.

pre-pro.com Distillery Database. "City Directory Listings Database." https://www.pre-pro.com/City/index.htm.

———. "Warehouse Records for RD#2, RD#10, RD#13 and RD#20 (WA)." https://www.pre-pro.com/midacore/list_warehouses.php?state=WA.

Quartz Mountain Distillers. https://quartzmountaindistillers.com.

Rasmussen, Ashley. Email interview, February 16, 2023.

Risen, Clay. "American Single Malt, a Freewheeling Cousin of Scotch, Comes of Age." *New York Times,* April 17, 2023.

Roberts, Kim. Email interview, March 5, 2023.

Rorabaugh, W.J. *The Alcoholic Republic: An American Tradition.* New York: Oxford University Press, 1979.

———. "The Origins of the Washington State Liquor Control Board, 1934." *Pacific Northwest Quarterly* 100, no. 4 (Fall 2009), 159–68. https://www.jstor.org/stable/40492243.

———. *Prohibition: A Concise History.* New York: Oxford University Press, 2018.

Sagawa, Kati. Email correspondence, November 7, 2023. https://thecraftdistrict.com/directory/percival-creek.

Salmon-Safe. https://salmonsafe.org.

Scarsella, Liana. "Bainbridge Organic Distillers Introduces the World's First Non-Japanese Whiskey Aged Exclusively in Virgin Japanese Mizunara Casks." *SIP,* March 28, 2016. https://sipmagazine.com/bainbridge-organic-distillers-introduces-the-worlds-first-non-japanese-whiskey-aged-exclusively-in-virgin-japanese-mizunara-casks.

Schefers, Audrey. Email interview, May 3, 2023.

Schiro, Paul V. Email interview, February 26, 2023.

Schrad, Mark Lawrence. *Smashing the Liquor Machine: A Global History of Prohibition.* New York: Oxford University Press, 2021.

Schwantes, Carlos Arnald. *The Pacific Northwest: An Interpretive History.* Lincoln: University of Nebraska Press, 2014.

Schwartz, Trish. Email interview, May 4, 2023.

Seattle Municipal Archives. "Prohibition in Seattle." https://www.seattle.gov/cityarchives/exhibits-and-education/digital-document-libraries/prohibition-in-seattle.

Seattle Municipal Archives Digital Collections. "Seattle at 150. Chapter 1: Foundations (1869–1896)." http://archives.seattle.gov/digital-collections/index.php/Gallery/281.

Seattle Times. "Liquor Control Board Getting New Name, More Pot Control." May 25, 2015. https://www.seattletimes.com/seattle-news/marijuana/liquor-control-board-getting-new-name-more-pot-control.

Silva, Elsa. Phone interview, March 9, 2023.

Skagit County Historical Society. Email correspondence, March 3, 2023.

Skagit River Journal. "Otto Peterson of Marblemount, Moonshine Marketing and Early Skagit River Life." Revised July 29, 2005. http://www.skagitriverjournal.com/Upriver/Cascades/Marblemount/PetersonOtto.html.

Skunk Brothers Spirits. http://skunkbrothersspirits.com.

Skybound Spirits. https://www.skyboundspirits.com.

Smiley, Jacqueline (KCSA Strategic Communications). Email interview, May 8, 2023.

Smith Tower. "Characters Exhibit Experience." https://www.smithtower.com/exhibits.

Snopes.com. "Shot of Whiskey." https://www.snopes.com/fact-check/shot-whiskey-origin.

Soden, Dale. "Matthews, Reverend Mark (1867–1940)." HistoryLink.org, January 13, 2007. https://historylink.org/File/8049.

———. "The Woman's Christian Temperance Union in the Pacific Northwest: The Battle for Cultural Control." *Pacific Northwest Quarterly* 94, no. 4 (Fall 2003), 197–207. https://www.jstor.org/stable/40491692.

Soule, Jake. Email interview, April 11, 2023.

Sound Spirits. "sound.spirits." https://www.instagram.com/p/By-yJNFAyMn.

Spokesman-Review. "How Many Craft Distilleries Are There in Washington State?" January 30, 2012. https://www.spokesman.com/blogs/officehours/2012/jan/30/how-many-craft-distilleries-are-there-washington-state.

Statista.com. "Number of Operating Craft Distilleries in the United States in 2021, by State." https://www.statista.com/statistics/463440/us-number-of-operating-craft-distilleries-by-state.

Stock, Mark. "Alcohol Brands and B-Corp Certification: Who Is Doing It and Why?" *The Manual*, October 21, 2019. https://www.themanual.com/food-and-drink/alcohol-companies-b-corp-certification.

Stranahan's. "How It Began: Born of Fire & Friendship." https://stranahans.com/about.

Stursa, Scott. *Distilled in Oregon*. Charleston, SC: The History Press, 2017.

Swede Hill Distilling. https://swedehilldistilling.com.

Temple, AJ. Phone interview, March 6, 2023, and in-person visit, May 9, 2023.

Tognetti, Skip. Phone interview, May 4, 2023.

Troth, Ernest. Email interview, May 5, 2023.

Troy, Eric. "Origin of Word 'Hooch' for Liquor." CulinaryLore, September 29, 2012. https://culinarylore.com/drinks:origin-of-the-word-hooch-for-liquor.

———. "'There's No Such Thing as a Free Lunch' Origin." CulinaryLore, November 27, 2016. https://culinarylore.com/food-history:no-such-thing-as-a-free-lunch.

Twain, Mark. *Life on the Mississippi*. Boston: James R. Osgood, 1883.

Varney, Philip. *Ghost Towns of the Pacific Northwest: Your Guide to the Hidden History of Washington, Oregon, and British Columbia*. Beverly, MA: Voyageur Press, 2013.

Voelsgen, Mhairi. Email correspondence, November 14, 2023.

Walker, Anna Sloan. "History of the Liquor Laws of the State of Washington." *Washington Quarterly*, January 6, 2010.

Warren, Nick. Email interview, April 3, 2023.

Washington Distillers Guild. https://washingtondistillersguild.org.

Washington Secretary of State. "Initiative Measure No. 1183, Washington State." https://www2.sos.wa.gov/elections/initiatives/text/i1183.pdf.

Washington State Archives. "Collection of Bankruptcy Papers for Overholtzer and Scott, 1870–1871."

Washington State Legislature. "RCW 66.44.140 Unlawful Sale, Transportation of Spirituous Liquor Without Stamp or Seal—Unlawful Operation, Possession of Still or Mash." https://apps.leg.wa.gov/rcw/default.aspx?Cite=66.

———. "SB 5448 - 2023-24: Concerning Liquor Licensee Privileges for the Delivery of Alcohol." https://app.leg.wa.gov/billsummary?BillNumber=5448&Chamber=Senate&Year=2023.

Washington State Liquor and Cannabis Board (LCB). "Added Activities for Distilleries, Wineries and Breweries." https://lcb.wa.gov/publications/licensing/forms/LIQ-1266-Added-Activities-Distilleries.docx.

———. "Distillery FAQ." https://lcb.wa.gov/enforcement/distillery-faq.

———. "Fact Sheet: Craft Distilleries License." https://lcb.wa.gov/publications/Leg_FactSheets/20080417factsheets08session/SHB2959.pdf.

———. "Farmers Market Authorization/Endorsement." https://lcb.wa.gov/licensing/farmers-market-authorizationendorsement.

———. "Retail Liquor Licenses and Endorsement Description and Fees Information." https://lcb.wa.gov/sites/default/files/publications/licensing/forms/LIQ-180-Retail-Liquor_License-Endorsement-Descriptions-and-Fees2.docx.

WashingtonVotes.org. "2008 House Bill 2959: Concerning Craft Distilleries." https://www.washingtonvotes.org/2008-HB-2959.

WA Wine. "History." https://www.washingtonwine.org/history.

Watt, Dan. Phone interview, May 6, 2023.

Waugh, Kathleen. "Guide to the Records of the Washington State Liquor Control Board: 1934–1993." Office of the Secretary of State Division of Archives and Records Management. Olympia, Washington, September 1999.

Weber/Roochvarg, Lynn. "One Day Before Friday Harbor in San Juan County Votes to Be 'Wet' or 'Dry,' Noted Anti-Liquor Evangelist Billy Sunday Comes to Preach on May 9, 1910." HistoryLink.org, October 9, 2016. https://www.historylink.org/File/20156.

Wheelhouse Distillery. https://www.yelp.com/biz/wheelhouse-distillery-anacortes.

Wilkinson, Eric. "Liquor Won't Be Sold in Smaller Grocery Stores After Washington Bill Fails." King5.com, February 11, 2020. https://www.king5.com/article/news/politics/washington-bill-could-allow-for-booze-sales-in-small-stores/281-905987fe-d418-4a6c-a5aa-40c7c6bc7b9f.

Williams, Mark. Email correspondence, November 12, 2023.

Wohlfert, John. Phone interview, May 4, 2023.

Women's Cocktail Collective. https://www.womenscocktailcollective.com.

Wood, Jennifer M. "15 Fun Phrases Popularized During Prohibition." *Mental Floss*, December 5, 2018. https://www.mentalfloss.com/article/54076/15-fun-phrases-were-popularized-during-prohibition.

Woodinville Whiskey Company. https://www.woodinvillewhiskeyco.com.

ABOUT THE AUTHOR

Becky Garrison is a journalist and author. Since moving to the Pacific Northwest in 2014, she has been covering the PNW craft culture, including food, beer, wine, spirits, cider and cannabis/CBD, as well as the regional festival scene and the rise of secular spiritual communities. Follow her travels via Instagram @Becky_Garrison or Facebook at BeckyGarrisonWriter.

Visit us at
www.historypress.com